The trucks and other vehicles from the major motion picture

Owner's Workshop Manual

© Haynes Publishing 2017

TM & © 2017 Paramount Pictures. All rights reserved.

Published in January 2017

A catalogue record for this book is available from the
British Library

ISBN 978 0 85733 805 1

Library of Congress catalog card no. 2014953500

Haynes Publishing, Sparkford, Yeovil,
Somerset BA22 7JJ, UK
Tel: 01963 440635
Int tel: +44 1963 440635
Website: www.haynes.com

Haynes North America, Inc.,
859 Lawrence Drive, Newbury Park,
California 91320, USA

Haynes Publishing
Author Ryder Windham
Illustration Ian Moores
Commissioning Editor Steve Rendle
Design Richard Parsons

Printed and bound in the UK by
Gomer Press, Llandysul Enterprise Park,
Llandysul, Ceredigion SA44 4JL

Paramount Pictures Licensing
Brand Manager, Product Development Sabi Lofgren
RHK Creative Services Risa Kessler

MONSTER TRUCKS

Haynes ®

he trucks and other vehicles from the major motion picture

Owner's Workshop Manual

By **Ryder Windham**   Illustrator **Ian Moores**

CONTENTS

INTRODUCTION BY MEREDITH

If you're reading this, I'm afraid the situation with the creatures has gotten completely out of control. What if some Terravex Oil workers have identified me and my friends to a government agency that wants to go after the creatures? Or someone found out my friends and I knew about the creatures beforehand. Maybe Terravex Oil is trying to sue us. Would they threaten to take away my family's house? I can only imagine, but I have a pretty vivid imagination.

Anyway, whatever the reasons, I'm afraid things have gotten worse. I really don't like being unprepared for anything. So I convinced my friends – those few people I know who also encountered the creatures – that we needed some evidence, a record of what happened, to protect ourselves. Convincing all of them wasn't easy (I'm thinking of *you*, Tripp Coley!), but finally, we all agreed to gather information. We also wrote about our own personal experiences with the creatures as well as certain representatives of Terravex Oil. We took some photos ourselves, and others came from security cameras, which may not have been exactly legal. I think it's best if I leave it at that.

But this record isn't just for us. Our big concern is for the creatures and their safety! We just want to protect them. Okay, at first, Tripp seemed more interested in using one as an engine for his truck, but even he came around.

Now that I think about it, perhaps something *good* came from all of this. Maybe the creatures aren't a secret anymore, and the world is okay with that. If that's true, it would be fantastic!

Or maybe Tripp wasn't joking when he said he was going to send all our notes and photos to Haynes Manuals so other people would know how to handle "monster trucks!"

But I can't believe Tripp would really do that. I mean, he's not stupid, right?

MEREDITH

That's Tripp's truck parked outside the barn on my family's property. Looks normal enough, doesn't it? Like any old heap outside a barn in North Dakota? This is a major case of looks being deceiving!
Meredith

I don't know where to begin. I'm no writer. I'm just a guy from North Dakota who likes to work on cars.

But I appreciate Meredith's idea for us to write down stuff about what happened, her whole deal about needing "insurance" to keep Terravex and maybe even government agencies off our cases. I get her point. On the other hand, I also think maybe we should just keep things secret, that we shouldn't write anything down. Maybe it would be better for everyone that way, especially for the creatures' friends who may be still in danger.

Anyway, I'm not worried about me and my family as much as I'm concerned about, well, friends. And not the ones above ground. I mean the underground friends. Not that they're only underground because they can live above ground too.

I just re-read what I wrote so far. Then I stared at my computer screen for five minutes straight.

This is goofy. I still don't know where to begin. I just called Meredith. She said I should start by introducing myself. There's not much to tell. My name's Tripp Coley. I live with my mom. She's a waitress. Her boyfriend is a cop. My parents are divorced. I go to Montgomery High School. Big deal.

So I guess I'm trying to say that my life isn't that unusual. I mean, it wasn't unusual until recently.

I know Meredith says we have to do this, but I'm not that good with words. I'm better at working on cars.

But I know this is important, and not just because Meredith told me, plus Mr. Weathers and Bill Dowd, at least fifty times. Oh, and Sam Geldon. He's in on this too. Unless we make some kind of record about what happened, how else are people going to know that the creatures aren't a threat?

TRIPP

I just called Meredith. She said I should start by introducing myself.

Tripp

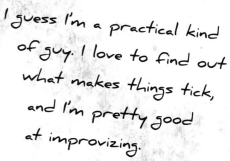

I guess I'm a practical kind of guy. I love to find out what makes things tick, and I'm pretty good at improvizing.

Tripp

' I KNOW MEREDITH SAYS WE HAVE TO DO THIS, BUT I'M NOT THAT GOOD WITH WORDS. I'M BETTER AT WORKING ON CARS'

My family has lived on a farm on the outskirts of Anderson in Sentinel County for generations. It doesn't seem that long ago, I was in elementary school, wondering what I'd do when I grew up, and where I should move to get a job. Before the oil boom, jobs were few and far between in Anderson.

Oil was first discovered in and around Anderson in the 1950s, but it wasn't until decades later that oil companies figured out how to get to the oil by way of horizontal drilling and hydraulic fracturing. Over the past ten years, Anderson has gone from a sleepy town to an oil-boom town, with more new job opportunities than anyone anticipated. And a considerable number of landowners have become very rich. That's because those particular landowners don't just own the land, but also have the mineral rights to everything below their property.

If you're not from around here, you might assume that every landowner owns mineral rights, but that's not true. Many farmers sold their mineral rights back in the 1930s, during the Great Depression, because they needed the money, and had no reason to imagine the mineral rights would ever be valuable.

When Terravex Energy realized how much oil was under Sentinel County, they began signing landowners to drilling leases. Some of these landowners became millionaires within a year after signing their contracts with Terravex. Although that's made the newly rich families happy, all the money that's flooded into Anderson has also brought problems. There's a housing shortage, and most rents have more than doubled. And then there are all the natural gas flares that have changed our landscape. Some people call it "progress," but Terravex has done tremendous damage to the environment. It has to stop!

MEREDITH

Tripp's mom, Cindy works at Red Hots, a restaurant in Anderson. I've heard that it's a favorite place for oil workers. I hope they tip well because Tripp's mother is really nice.

Meredith, why did you write about my mom? She didn't have anything to do with Creatch.

Tripp

SHE RAISED YOU, DIDN'T SHE? HA HA!

MEREDITH

I took this photo not far from my house. Sentinel County still has a lot of lovely areas. Unfortunately, Terravex doesn't care much about beautiful views.

Meredith

'ANDERSON LOOKS PRETTY MUCH THE SAME AS IT DID WHEN I WAS LITTLE, BUT THERE ARE A LOT OF NEW APARTMENT BUILDINGS AT THE EDGE OF TOWN TO ACCOMMODATE ALL THE OIL WORKERS'

Tripp and I go to Montgomery High School in Anderson. I want to go to college and major in either biology or zoology, depending on where I go. I was recently partnered with Tripp on a school project. I was trying to get hold of him when I saw him outside the dealership.

But I'm sad to say I don't have many friends here. Years ago, up through fourth grade, I was best friends with Brianna, but that was before her family hit it big with an oil lease for their land. I guess for some people, coming into a lot of money just makes them feel superior to others, and gives them an excuse to buy expensive cars and trucks! I'm really not bitter about the fact that my family didn't profit in any way from Terravex, but I don't like the way the influx of money has changed so many people and created so much friction in Anderson.

MEREDITH

I mentioned my former friend Brianna. She's the blonde girl in the sun dress. The boy standing next to her is Jake, her boyfriend, and they're standing in front of his truck. What is it with guys and their trucks?

Meredith

MONTGOMERY
HIGH SCHOOL

'TRIPP AND I GO TO MONTGOMERY HIGH SCHOOL IN ANDERSON.
IT'S A GOOD SCHOOL AND I'M DOING WELL IN ALL MY CLASSES'

MYSTERIOUS VANDALS

My name is Sam Geldon. I'm a senior at Montgomery High School, and my Dad runs the local Dodge dealership. Recently we've had some trouble with a few jerks vandalizing the premises – nothing serious, but nobody wants broken windows!

One morning it suddenly looked as if the jerks had stepped it up. A truck on its side, others shoved out of the way, and, weirdly, the gas tanks ripped clean out of some of the trucks! I mean, why? There are easier ways to steal gas!

Anyway, that's when I first began to get to know Tripp a little better. Sure, I knew who he was, and I'd seen him around school, but nothing more than that.

After the crazy events with the gas-tank vandals, a few students from Montgomery High gathered to see what was going on, along with police cars and a news crew, when Tripp arrived on the scene. I was talking to Meredith, when he came over to ask what had happened. When I explained about the truck gas tanks, he went straight on over to take a look, and off went Meredith too – she seemed like she needed to talk to Tripp...

Later, when Tripp turned up at the dealership to ask if he could use the custom shop, I wasn't so sure. Something told me it would all work out OK, but then we started chopping the Rebel – my 16th birthday present! Meredith and Mr. Weathers were with Tripp, and they seemed responsible. But how was I supposed to know Tripp wanted me to help him chop up trucks so they could be used by creatures?

Don't get me wrong though. Tripp didn't mislead me. No one did. I never imagined getting involved in something so crazy, but I'm glad I did.

Tripp said that when we finish these notes, we should send them to Haynes Manuals so they could make the information available to other people.

Monster Trucks Owner's Workshop Manual. Heck, I'd want to read that book. Who wouldn't?

SAM

I used to think that stories about Bigfoot and the Loch Ness Monster were totally bogus until I saw creatures with my own eyes. It's true, I really did see creatures. No question about it. And now I can't help wondering if maybe there's some truth to those other stories.

Sam

Heads up! It's Sentinel County CSI! I give Sheriff Rick Lovick – I call him Rick – a hard time for two reasons: he's my mom's boyfriend, and he keeps his car way too clean. I swear, he must wash that car daily, and dusts it hourly, maybe even more often on a slow day. Oh, I forgot, he's always on my case about going to college. So that gives me three reasons to give him a hard time.

Rick's latest set of wheels is a 2014 Jeep Cherokee. It's what the manufacturers call a mid-size "crossover utility vehicle," or a CUV, because it's sort of somewhere between a sport utility vehicle – an SUV, in case you didn't know already – and a station wagon. I kid him about how clean it is all the time.

Even though we don't always get on, Rick's okay. Maybe I even appreciate that he thinks I should go to college. But don't tell him I said that. What I really appreciate is that when my friends and I most needed his help, he was there for us.

TRIPP

SHERIFF RICK
WITH TRIPP'S MOM.
MEREDITH

DUL!

Sheriff's Office Gets New Vehicles

The Sentinel County Sheriff's Office has acquired new vehicles to improve its presence on the streets and meet the needs of the community. Sheriff Rick Lovick announced that the combination of State funds and support from the Sentinel County Commission are supporting the acquisition of 10 new vehicles, including a 2014 Jeep Cherokee that will serve as Lovick's patrol vehicle. Four previously commissioned patrol vehicles are expected to be kept on, which means the Sheriff's Office will have a total of 14 vehicles at their disposal.

Jim Pattison Chrysler-Dodge-Jeep dealership of Anderson won the bid for the new vehicles, which are sufficient to provide 14 deputies with "home cars." According to Lovick, "By taking vehicles home, deputies won't have to wait for transportation during shift change. We'll also be able to mobilize more units faster, while increasing our visible presence in the county."

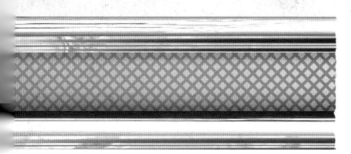

Even though we don't always get along, Rick's okay. Maybe I even appreciate that he thinks I should go to college. But don't tell him I said that.

Tripp

TRIPP'S BIKE

I built my bike from parts I salvaged at Weathers' Scrap Yard. I've been working for Mr. Weathers for a while now, and he's a great guy, lets me use his tools and everything. He's also taught me more about welding than I ever learned in the high school auto shop. Anyway, Meredith suggested I write about my bike because... I can't remember why. Something about "illustrating my mechanical ability," or whatever, so people know that the monster truck wasn't the first thing I ever worked on.

At a glance, the bike looks beat up, but it's actually very solid. The frame is titanium, made by Brodie, a Canadian company, and it has the original Shimano groupset. It's an expensive bike, so I felt lucky when I found the pieces in the scrap yard. I'm guessing it belonged to someone with more money than sense. The gears were jammed, but that was an easy fix. It amazes me, all the good stuff that people throw away. One of the tires was shredded, so I replaced both with WTB knobbly tires.

I installed the shock absorber, and I'll be the first to admit it's not pretty. The welds are solid, just not much to look at. Still, it's durable, and definitely a smoother ride than you'd get from the average off-the-rack bike.

TRIPP

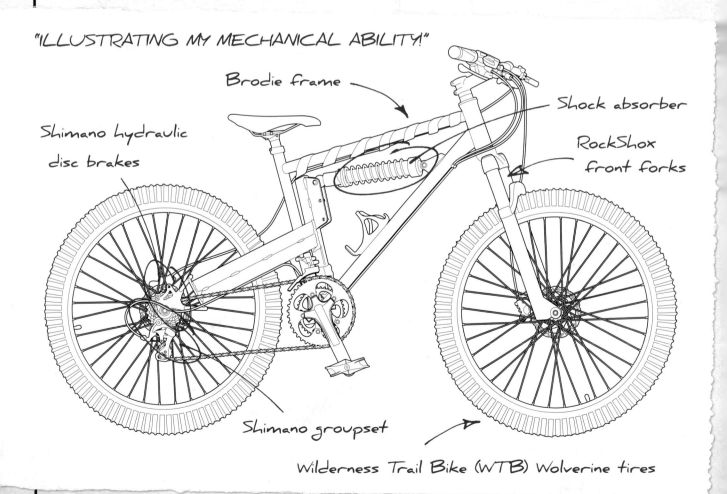

"ILLUSTRATING MY MECHANICAL ABILITY!"

Brodie frame

Shock absorber

RockShox front forks

Shimano hydraulic disc brakes

Shimano groupset

Wilderness Trail Bike (WTB) Wolverine tires

It's durable, and definitely a smoother ride than you'd get from the average off-the-rack bike.

'I'LL BE THE FIRST TO ADMIT IT'S NOT PRETTY. THE WELDS ARE SOLID, JUST NOT MUCH TO LOOK AT'

I know some people will probably laugh at me for saying this, but Weathers' Scrap Yard is probably my favorite place in North Dakota. Granted, there's a lot of North Dakota I haven't seen, and most of the world that I'll probably never see. But I never get tired of being at Mr. Weathers' place. I imagine most folks look at a scrap yard and all they see is a lot of junk, or they look at a wrecked car and they think: "That's the end of that." Me, I don't see useless junk. I see raw materials for making new things.

If it weren't for the scrap yard, and all the tips Mr. Weathers has given me about cutting, and welding, also how to fabricate parts, I doubt I would have had any idea about how to help the creatures.

TRIPP

If it weren't for the scrap yard I doubt I would have had any idea about how to help the creatures.

Tripp

WEATHERS'
PICK-A-PART
USED CARS AND PARTS
CALL: 701-015-4794

People just call me Weathers. I own Weathers' Pick-A-Part Used Cars and Parts, Weathers' Scrap Yard and Weathers' Welding Shop. They're all on the same property.

It was by way of the security cameras that I got my first sight of Creatch. I'm glad for that because if I'd met Creatch up close the way Tripp did, I can only imagine how I might have reacted. My usual way of dealing with varmints is with a rifle, but I've never encountered a gas-guzzling varmint with tentacles before. I like to think I would have worked out that Creatch was intelligent, like Tripp did, but I can only imagine. Still, got to say, Tripp Coley's a good kid, a good young man. And anyone who thinks "there's no such thing as monsters" has another think coming.

WEATHERS

MR. WEATHERS' TOW TRUCK

Mr. Weathers' tow truck is a Dodge D-500, which is around 50 years old, and built like a tank! He's made a bunch of modifications so it's accessible for his wheelchair, and he's also installed hand-controls for acceleration and braking.

The truck still has the original engine, a 225 Premium Slant-Six. According to an old brochure Mr. Weathers keeps in his shop, the engine has "many heavy-duty features to give exceptional ruggedness and long life. Among them are a roller timing chain, tough bi-metal connecting rod bearings, heat-resistant Stellite-faced exhaust valves, Roto-Caps to protect the exhaust valves from carbon build-up, and Polyacrylic valve stem seals to prevent oil loss." Given the truck's age and the fact that it's still rolling, I think it's clear that Mr. Weathers knows how to keep machines running.

Although Mr. Weathers primarily uses the tow truck for hauling stalled or wrecked cars, he also works with insurance companies and uses it for repossessions. His truck sure came in handy when we needed a vehicle large enough for a monstrous friend. More on that later.

TRIPP

The truck's towing gear is pretty heavy duty, just like our friend Creatch!!

Tripp

CAR COMPACTOR

Mr. Weathers' car compactor, better known as the crusher, is on a flatbed, making it portable, but it's been resting on the same spot in the scrap yard since I can remember.

The way we use it – first, we strip the car of all working parts that can be refurbished and resold. We also remove the battery, the chemicals in the air-conditioning system, and the gas tank – all the stuff with hazardous materials. Then we remove the tires, which can be either resold or recycled. When the car's ready to be crushed, we use a forklift to load it into the crushing bed.

After that, it's just a matter of activating the hydraulics, and crushing the car as flat as possible so it takes up less space. That way, more crushed cars can be loaded onto trucks and sent to a recycler. Anyone who thinks of the crusher as a great big toy is just plain stupid. It can reduce anything – even a good-sized truck or a luxury limousine – to a flattened heap of metal, so just imagine what it could do to some rich idiot and his beer-guzzling friends. On second thought, don't imagine it. It's too messy.

I don't like to admit that I almost killed Creatch with the crusher, but that was when we first met. I thought it was trying to kill me, but we both held back. That's when I realized it was intelligent, that it was thoughtful. I'm pretty sure that Creatch realized the same thing about me at the same time.

TRIPP

Controls for the car compactor

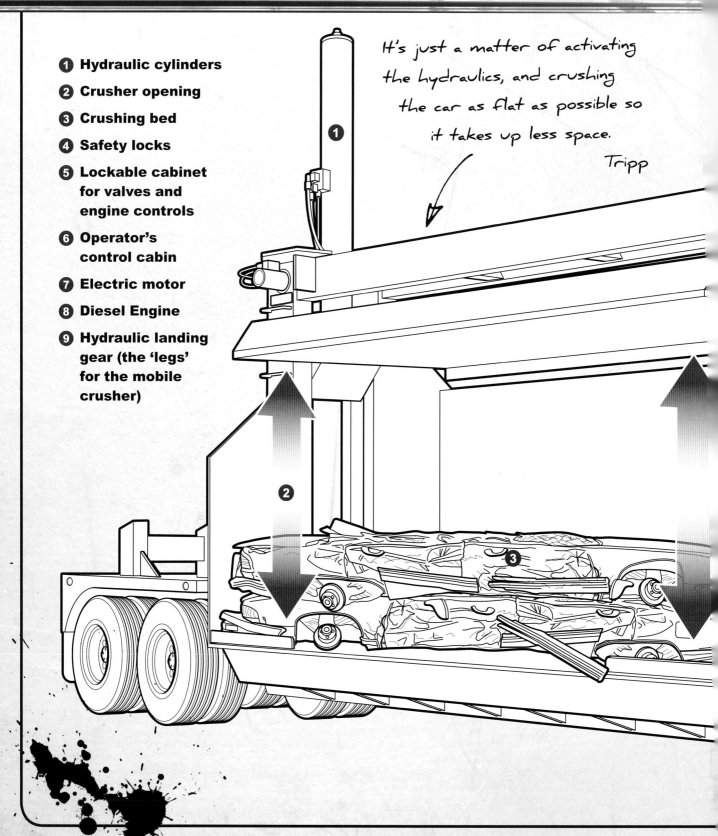

1. Hydraulic cylinders
2. Crusher opening
3. Crushing bed
4. Safety locks
5. Lockable cabinet for valves and engine controls
6. Operator's control cabin
7. Electric motor
8. Diesel Engine
9. Hydraulic landing gear (the 'legs' for the mobile crusher)

It's just a matter of activating the hydraulics, and crushing the car as flat as possible so it takes up less space.

Tripp

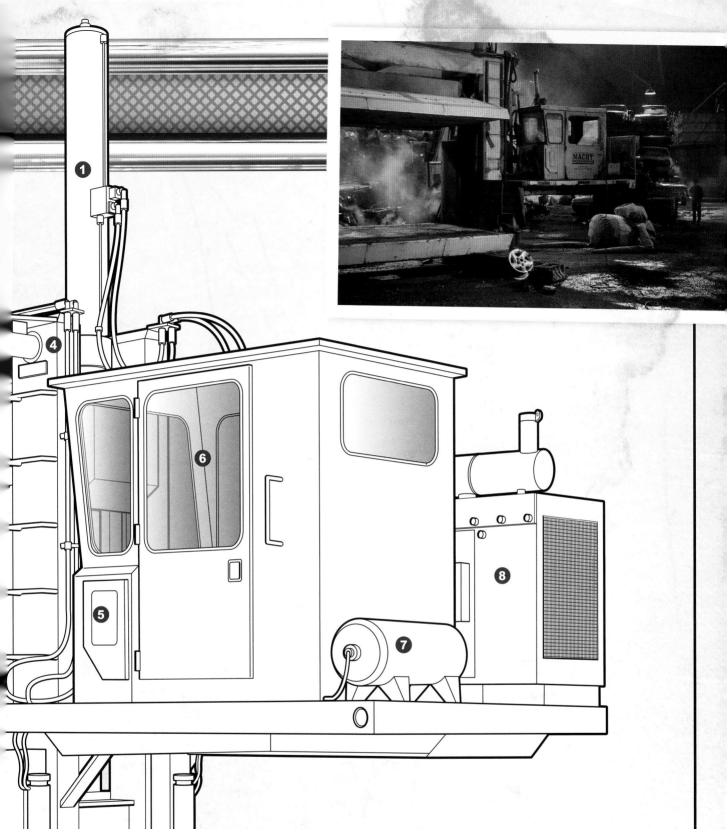

'ANYONE WHO REGARDS THE CRUSHER AS A GREAT
BIG TOY IS JUST PLAIN STUPID. IT CAN REDUCE
ANYONE FROM A GOOD-SIZED TRUCK TO A LUXURY
LIMOUSINE INTO A FLATTENED HEAP OF METAL'

THE OLD MUTT

The Old Mutt was what Mr. Weathers and I called the remains of a Dodge C-Series pickup truck from the 1950s. I don't know how long it had been lying in the scrap yard. It was covered with more dust than rust, but was still in a sad state, and its engine was a goner. I asked Mr. Weathers why he hadn't crushed it. He said he thought enough of it was solid that it could be a good project for a restoration or a hot rod, and he was just waiting for the right fool to come along to make him an offer. I said, "What if the fool doesn't have any money?" He laughed at that, told me he was just joking, said if I could get the Old Mutt running and get it out of his scrap yard, I'd have myself a pickup. Nice, huh?

From what I've read about the C-Series, Dodge put a lot of innovations into this truck. It had a new frame design so it could turn tighter, and the cab sits lower on the frame, making it easier to get in and out. The single-piece curved windshield appeared in 1955, and gave better visibility for the driver. The C-Series came with a 110-horsepower 230cu in L-6 engine, but buyers had the choice to get a 241cu in V8 – the first V8 engine for Dodge. Other options included a fully automatic PowerFlite transmission and an overdrive for fuel economy.

I made a few modifications. I installed a Sidewinder lockout shifter, which has safety features to prevent jamming or any accidental shifting. It's also super rugged. And I put in Eibach shocks that I removed from a totaled truck. I'd been planning on dropping in a 6.4 liter Hemi V8 that Mr. Weathers said I could have, but that was before the creatures came along.

TRIPP

made a few
modifications,
including fitting
Eibach shocks!
Tripp

THE OLD MUTT

Mr. Weathers has what he calls his "library," a collection of automotive maintenance manuals and promotional brochures. Digging through the library, I found a bunch of pictures and info about the original Dodge C-Series truck. Looking at the Old Mutt now, it's almost hard to believe the truck was once factory-fresh – that it started off so clean and sharp.

I'm guessing over the years the Old Mutt changed owners a few times. Maybe I'll do some research, see if I can dig up info about the previous owners, find out if any are still alive. I'd love to see the looks on their faces, if they could see what I've done with their former property!

TRIPP

The Old Mutt's rear axle was a little noisy, so I checked the Shop Manual for clues I never did manage to check out the gears though!

DODGE
"Job-Rated"
TRUCKS

SHOP MANUAL

C-3 Series (After)
All Models

I was glad the PowerFlite transmission seemed to be working — it looked a little complicated to fix!

Tripp

Fig. 5—Checking Gear Lash at End of Universal Yoke

and differential assembly out on support to permit installation of pinion and cage assembly.

10. INSTALLING PINION AND CAGE ASSEMBLY

(1) Install gasket coated with non-hardening sealing compound over studs and install pinion cage assembly, aligning lubricating holes. Tap assembly into position with a soft mallet.

(2) Install pinion cage cover (with new seals) and tighten to 58 foot-pounds torque.

(3) Install universal joint yoke, washer and nut. Using holding Tool C-949 and torque wrench Tool DD-994, tighten to 400 foot-pounds torque.

(4) Install thrust block in cover housing half. Position ring gear and differential assembly in case half. Make sure gasket is in place and install cover half of housing with six equally spaced and evenly tightened bolts to 45 foot-pounds torque.

11. CHECKING GEAR LASH

(1) Attach dial indicator (Tool C-430) to pinion, cage stud (Fig. 5). Position indicator against yoke two (2) inches from center of pinion shaft. Gear lash should be from .013 to .033 inch.

(2) Where backlash is outside of specifications, transpose spacers from one side of ring gear and differential assembly to the other.

(3) After establishing proper gear lash, install remaining bolts and tighten to 72 foot-pounds torque.

12. ASSEMBLE AXLE SHAFTS AND STEERING KNUCKLES

(1) A new felt washer should be installed in the steering knuckle companion flanges to insure

against oil leakage and the entry of dirt into the universal joint. Assemble each end of the axle as follows: Make sure that drive shaft oil seal is in place in axle housing. Place the steering knuckle companion flange in position on the trunion and attach the trunion in position to the axle housing.

(2) If universal drive has been separated from axle shaft, reassemble the parts, using a new drive shaft snap ring. Install the universal drive assembly.

(3) Bolt the steering knuckle flange to the companion flange. Install the upper and lower bearing cups and the bearing cones. Install the caps with the original shim packs and new gaskets.

(4) Replace the steering knuckle felt (oil seal) washer and the steering knuckle bushing. Install the steering knuckle, brake support and oil slinger.

(5) Install the steering knuckle spacer and felt over the end of the universal drive and install the spring.

(6) Install the wheel bearing inner bearing cone assembly on the knuckle and install the hub.

(7) Install outer wheel bearing cone and install the bearing adjusting nut. Adjust hub bearings by spinning the hub while tightening the adjusting nut until the hub will not turn. Loosen the nut so hub will turn easily with just a slight amount of end play. Install the lock ring and lock nut. Tighten lock nut. Retest adjustment to insure that wheel hub is free to rotate and then bend the lock washer over the flats of the lock nut in two places to secure the adjustment.

(8) Install the drive shaft flange using a new gasket. Install the shaft snap ring and reinstall the puller screws and screw lock nuts in the flange.

(9) Test adjustment of steering bearings by swinging the hub in both directions of rotation. A slight drag should be indicated when moving the hub. If the assembly turns too free, tighten the bearing adjustment of both upper and lower bearings by removing shims. Add shims if the assemblies require excessive effort to move. If shims are added to loosen the bearing fit, shake the assembly when the caps are removed, to move the bearing cups out against the caps and obtain the proper setting provided by the shims.

(10) When both ends of the axle are assembled, and properly adjusted, install the wheel, tires and tie rod assembly.

(11) Assemble the axle to the truck and adjust the tie rod to obtain 1/8 inch toe-in. Then check the wheel caster and camber angles.

(12) Fill axle housing with hypoid gear lubricant. Lubricate universal joints and steering knuckles.

AXLE REAR

SERVICE DIAGNOSIS
CONDITIONS—POSSIBLE CAUSES

13. REAR AXLE NOISE

Rear Axle noises are generally divided into three groups:

(1) *GEAR NOISE ON PULL*—If the noise is of a heavy pitch and increases as truck's speed is increased, it is an indication of scored teeth due to loss of lubricant, incorrent mesh of teeth or use of incorrect type lubricant.

(2) *GEAR NOISE ON COAST*—If noise is heavy and irregular, it is an indication of scored teeth which has resulted from excessive end play in pinion bearings or from incorrect adjustment.

(3) *BEARING NOISE ON PULL OR COAST*—Indicates rear pinion bearings are chipped, cracked, scored, badly worn and loose. Bearings that are badly worn, or broken will make a rough grating sound that may increase or decrease slightly in volume as speed changes.

14. DIFFERENTIAL CASE BREAKAGE

Possible Causes:

(1) Improper adjustment of differential bearings.

(2) Excessive ring gear clearance.

(3) Truck overloaded.

(4) Erratic clutch operation.

15. SCORING OF DIFFERENTIAL GEARS

Possible Causes:

(1) Insufficient lubrication.

(2) Improper grade of lubricant.

(3) Excessive spinning of one wheel.

16. TOOTH BREAKING (RING GEAR AND PINION)

Possible Causes:

(1) Overloading.

(2) Erratic clutch operation.

(3) Ice-spotted pavements.

(4) Improper adjustment.

17. LOSS OF LUBRICANT

Possible Causes:

(1) Lubricant level too high.

(2) Worn axle shaft oil seals.

(3) Cracked rear axle housing.

(4) Worn drive pinion oil seal or yoke.

AXLE REAR
(C3-HW)

DESCRIPTION OF C3-HW REAR AXLE

The rear axle is of the unit-type, in that the drive gear and pinion are mounted directly into the case half of the axle housing. The pinion is straddle mounted and has two tapered bearings in front of the pinion teeth and one radial bearing at the inner end.

18. REMOVING AXLE ASSEMBLY

(1) Remove plug from bottom of housing and drain lubricant. Disconnect propeller shaft universal

at axle pinion yoke end and brakes at "tee" connection on axle.

(2) Remove spring clip nuts and remove clips. Raise truck and roll axle out from under the truck.

19. INSTALLING ASSEMBLY

(1) Roll axle under truck. Lower truck until springs rest on spring seats, position springs and install spring clips and nuts. Tighten nuts to 69 foot-pounds.

(2) Connect brake tubes and propeller shaft.

(3) Bleed and adjust brakes.

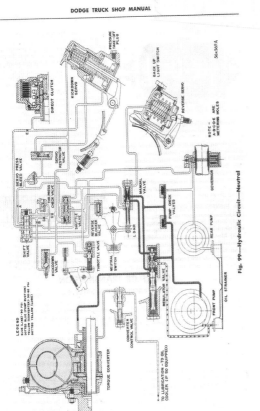

Fig. 99—Hydraulic Circuit—Neutral

Fig. 100—Hydraulic Circuit—Breakaway

ORIGINAL SCHEME

Even before I met Creatch, I actually considered transforming the Old Mutt into a monster truck. It wasn't my first idea. I was thinking of something more practical, or at least more practical for me, like a street-legal rat rod. Nothing too ridiculous, just a get-around-town car. But I also liked the idea of going off road in a monster truck, a true getaway vehicle. I thought it would be a kick to take off in any direction away from Anderson, and to keep driving until I reached a wall I couldn't climb.

Anyway, here's a sketch that I drew of the Old Mutt as a monster truck. I drew some other sketches too, played around with the paint job, and thought red would look good. I envisioned the truck having running lights, 2.5 Rochwell axles, front and rear hydraulic steering with toploaders, and 48x33 tires. It's pretty obvious I wasn't thinking about how much the project would cost, that I was just playing around. If money hadn't been any object, I can only imagine what I would have done with the Old Mutt!

TRIPP

Looking at this
sketch now,
I can't believe
I imagined the
Old Mutt could
be transformed
into a shiny toy!

In hindsight, I don't think a red paint
job would have been good — especially
as Terravex trucks are red!

How about those
tractor tires?
Okay, they're
not great for
high speeds, but
they look cool.

I already mentioned a few of Dodge's innovations when they introduced the C-Series truck – the new frame design for tighter turns, curved windshield for better visibility, PowerFlite transmission and so on. But I guess for Dodge fans and mechanics, the most significant and memorable thing about the C-Series is that they were the first Dodge trucks available with a V8 engine, with hemispherical – "Hemi" – combustion chambers. Chrysler developed the first Hemi engine during World War II, when they worked on the design of the engine for the Republic P-47 Thunderbolt fighter plane. Now you know.

After doing some research, I think the PowerFlite transmission also deserves a mention. Chrysler engineered and produced this two-speed automatic transmission system from 1954 to 1955, and from what I've read, its design is as simple as it is durable. One odd feature is that the PowerFlite transmission doesn't have a "Park" setting. To park your PowerFlite-equipped truck, you need to use the handbrake. That's because all Chrysler cars and trucks in the 1950s had wheel brakes that were independent from the parking brake. The C-Series truck's parking brake is mounted right behind the transmission, and locks the rear wheels the same way as the "Park" setting for other trucks. Still, some drivers today would probably be confused by how the PowerFlite system features the letters R-N-D-L (Reverse, Neutral, Drive, and Low) on the selector gate, but lacks P for "Park."

TRIPP

The cabin is comfortable, and the curved windshield provides excellent visibility.

The bumpers and grille bars are super solid. The whole truck was built to last.

1. Front bumper
2. Grille bars
3. 241cu in V8 engine
4. Windshield
5. Windshield visor
6. Rear fender extension
7. Rear bumper
8. Rear axle/differential unit
9. Propeller shaft
10. Front suspension
11. Road tyre
12. Headlamp

I know this is a little off topic for this "report" we're writing, but I just have to talk about this stuff. Even if you've never seen a monster truck show, you're probably aware of them from seeing ads promoting the events on TV. My mom took me to a show when I was little, and it was awesome, watching those enormous trucks race across the arena and also do stunts, like driving over cars and crushing them. But even as a kid, I could see that a lot of time and hard work went into building them, and I tried to learn as much as I could about their mechanical aspects. I mean, think about it... Monster trucks are a wicked blend of drag racer, dune buggy, and farm equipment. They're amazing.

One of the big names on the monster truck circuit is *Raminator*, which is 10-feet tall, weighs over 10,000 pounds, rides on 66-inch grooved racing tires, and is powered by a 565 cubic inch Supercharged Hemi that produces 2,000 horsepower. Last I checked, *Raminator* has been named the Monster Truck Racing Association's "Truck of the Year" eight times. *Raminator* also broke the world record for the fastest monster truck when it got up to 99.1mph over a quarter-mile stretch at Circuit of the Americas in Austin, Texas. The previous record was 96.8mph. In case you're wondering about fuel efficiency, for *Raminator*'s record-breaking run, it burned about five gallons of methanol, which translates to 264 feet per gallon.

And if you're wondering why I'm telling you so much about *Raminator*, it's just to point out that I'd been looking at monster trucks and thinking about them for years before I built one. Granted, mine was powered by a real monster, but still, I'm glad all that knowledge turned out to be good for something.

TRIPP

Tripp, do you just know all this info about Raminator, or did you have to look it up in a book?
MEREDITH

Book?
What's a book?
Tripp

Raminator in
Anderson! Geldon
Dodge has been
displaying Raminator
above the remains
of "the competiton."

RAM

RAMTRUCKS.COM

RAM

Originally founded as Terravex Oil in Texas in 1980, Terravex Energy is one of the most respected and experienced oil-well service companies in North America, with operations in Texas, North and South Dakota, Wyoming, and Montana. Also one of the fastest growing service companies in the petroleum industry, Terravex Energy specializes in the exploration, acquisition, development, and production of oil, and employs cutting-edge horizontal drilling and hydraulic fracturing technology.

Committed to safety as well as innovation, Terravex Energy always works in full compliance with federal commissions and environmental agencies, and is distinguished for utilizing pipelines and gas-capture technology to limit burn-off and collect natural gas, increasing revenue for natural gas as well as crude oil. Terravex Energy services range from fluid management and oil-well facilities construction to well-site support services and transport. Terravex Energy currently boasts a trucking fleet of nearly 500 trucks, and also contracts more than 1,000 drivers to transport oil, sand, water, and other products to the oilfield, making Terravex Energy trucks a familiar sight on our nation's highways.

For more information about joining the Terravex Energy family, visit our website or contact your local Terravex Energy representative today.

Terravex doesn't take the oil and run.
We're in it for the long haul.

My name is Bill Dowd. I'm a petroleum geologist, and I was the lead scientist at Terravex Energy for fifteen years, and worked directly under Reece Tenneson for most of that time. I was responsible for conducting the surveys and analyzing the data that confirmed the existence of oil deposits, including the substantial deposits in Sentinel County. Or as Tenneson used to say, I was Terravex's highest-paid treasure hunter. And I did it well. But as much as I liked being a "treasure hunter," the fact is that I was in the business of exploiting natural resources that can never be replenished. Now, I shamefully admit that I also occasionally manipulated data, that I presented information that would benefit Tenneson's career as well as my own, all in the name of money.

I can't correct all the mistakes I made, but I'd like to do whatever I can to help save and preserve the creatures that we unearthed at Pankeska Rock. If I can accomplish that much, then I'll have done some good.

Tenneson met me at the Pankeska Rock drilling site shortly after I discovered the water pocket above the oil that we'd targeted. Although finding water two miles below the surface was important scientifically, because it allowed the possibility of an ecosystem, Tenneson was only interested in getting the oil.

BILL DOWD

Terravex Executive at Pankeska Ridge

Terravex has assigned senior executive Reece Tenneson, to oversee oil-drilling operations at the Pankeska Ridge facility in Sentinel County. Tenneson has extensive experience managing Terravex operations throughout Texas, and his credentials also include negotiating and securing the lease agreements, titles and right-of-way accesses that were required for Terravex to build their facility at Pankeska Rock. "It's my privilege to work with Sentinel County's officials and citizens," Tenneson said in the release, "to help bring so many jobs to the beautiful state of North Dakota."

Terravex Energy Annual Report

Update: Pankeska Rock Facility

Using sophisticated technology to locate oil deposits over two miles beneath the Earth's surface, Terravex Energy's geological survey teams work closely with drill teams to reach the oil deposits with near pinpoint accuracy. Terravex employs highly qualified, fully trained professionals to oversee and carry out the labor-intensive process of oil extraction.

After a survey team determined a vast oil deposit beneath the Pankeska Rock site in North Dakota, Terravex crews drilled for a natural source of water for use during the oil-drilling process, and also dug a reserve pit for the disposal of rock cuttings and drilling mud. A drill truck dug the starter hole, which was subsequently lined with a steel conductor pipe. New sections of pipe were added as the hole became deeper.

The drilling rig was assembled above the starter hole, and cement and drill mud were pumped through the conductor pipe to create a cylindrical cement wall around the length of the hole, preventing the sides of the hole from caving in. After the cement hardened, it was thoroughly tested for hardness and alignment. The process of drilling, adding pipe, and pumping in cement and drill mud was repeated until reaching the targeted oil trap.

The drill team at Pankeska Rock uses advanced hydraulic fracturing techniques to reach and extract oil and gas. Water, proppant, and chemicals are pumped into the well at high pressure to fracture the rock and provide paths for gas and oil to escape and rise to the surface. The proppant consists mostly of sand and ceramic pellets – granular materials that fill cracks and "prop up" the well, helping to keep the fractures open as they maintain the well's structural integrity.

By extracting oil from Pankeska Rock, Terravex not only brings economic growth to North Dakota, but greatly improves America's energy independence.

TERRAVEX DOESN'T MENTION
THAT THE CHEMICALS IN
THE FRACKING FLID MAY
INCLUDE ACIDS AND
OXYGEN SCAVENGERS,
OR THAT EVERY FRACKING
OPERATION REQUIRES MILLIONS
OF GALLONS OF WATER!

MEREDITH

Meredith, you're correct, fracturing
fluid is typically made up from
90 per cent water, 9.5 per cent
sand, and 0.5 per cent chemicals,
and the chemicals are similar to
what's found in household cleaning
supplies. Before I discovered the
existence of the creatures, I never
had reason to consider whether my
work affected any life forms that
far beneath the ground. I'm not
making excuses for my work or
trying to diminish your concerns,
just offering more info.

Bill Dowd

This diagram of the drilling facility at Pankeska Rock is a typical set-up for Terravex Energy. Building such a facility takes three to five months: a few weeks to prepare the site, four to six weeks to drill the well, and one to three months of what's called "completion activities" – mostly checking and double-checking all the apparatus, data, etc – and then up to another week for stimulation, the process of pumping stimulation fluid into the well bore to cause fracturing. The stimulation fluid consists of 99.5% water and sand, and 0.5% of a combination of special chemicals. Terravex invested in the Pankeska Rock facility with the prospect that production could last 20 to 40 years.

BILL DOWD

1. **Engines**
2. **Fluid pump**
3. **Sand storage tanks**
4. **Treater manifold**
5. **Well head**
6. **Drill rig**
7. **Crown block**
8. **Derrick**
9. **Driller's shack**
10. **Fluid hose**
11. **Fluid storage tanks**

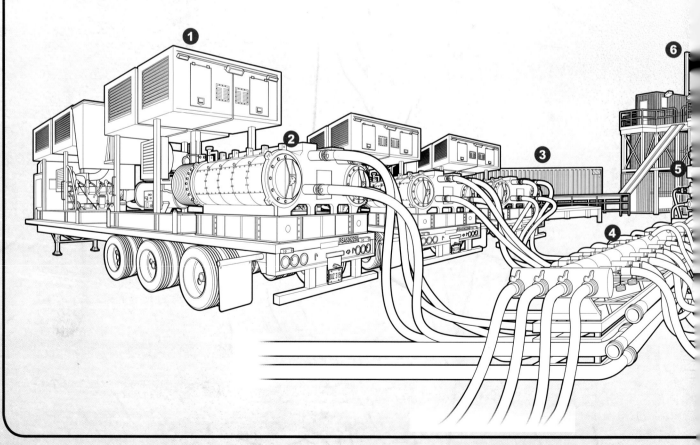

TERRAVEX FACILITIES CERTAINLY LOOK
NEAT AND TIDY BEFORE EVERYTHING
GOES HORRIBLY WRONG!

MEREDITH

Oil production is up in the United States. This increased productivity can be largely attributed to improvements in drilling technology that make it economically feasible to extract oil from previously inaccessible deposits. Terravex is at the forefront of these improvements, and holds numerous patents for contemporary drilling equipment and drill components.

Terravex drilling facilities utilize the most technologically advanced drills and techniques. Our drill bits use the sheer rotary power of Polycrystalline Diamond Cutters (PDC) to cut through rock formations. To craft these cutters, premium saw-grade diamond crystals are fused together under high-pressure, high-temperature conditions in the presence of a tungsten carbide catalytic metal.

Terravex uses extended-reach drills, which travel outward as well as down. Drilling engineers use magnetometers and inclinometers to control the position and angle of the wellbore. After sending drilling fluid into the wellbore, pressure pulses send data back to the drill team for analysis. The team uses this data to create 3-D imagery of the layers of rock and the locations of the oil, allowing them to pre-map their target and reach it with remarkable accuracy.

Most equipment failures are caused by vibrational phenomena, including torsional "stick-slip," which is caused by irregular friction between the drill-bit and the rock surface, and by "bit bounce," which causes the drill-bit to intermittently lose contact with the rock surface. Controlling such vibrations is crucial to prevent damage to equipment and to the oil well itself. Terravex uses drills designed to minimize vibrations, reducing the chance of damage.

To give the team an extra advantage in case they encounter unexpected obstacles, the drill is also equipped with an armored camera and lighting system that transmit views of whatever lies in the drill's path. Terravex shareholders can be assured that the drill team always aims to see crude oil, and plenty of it.

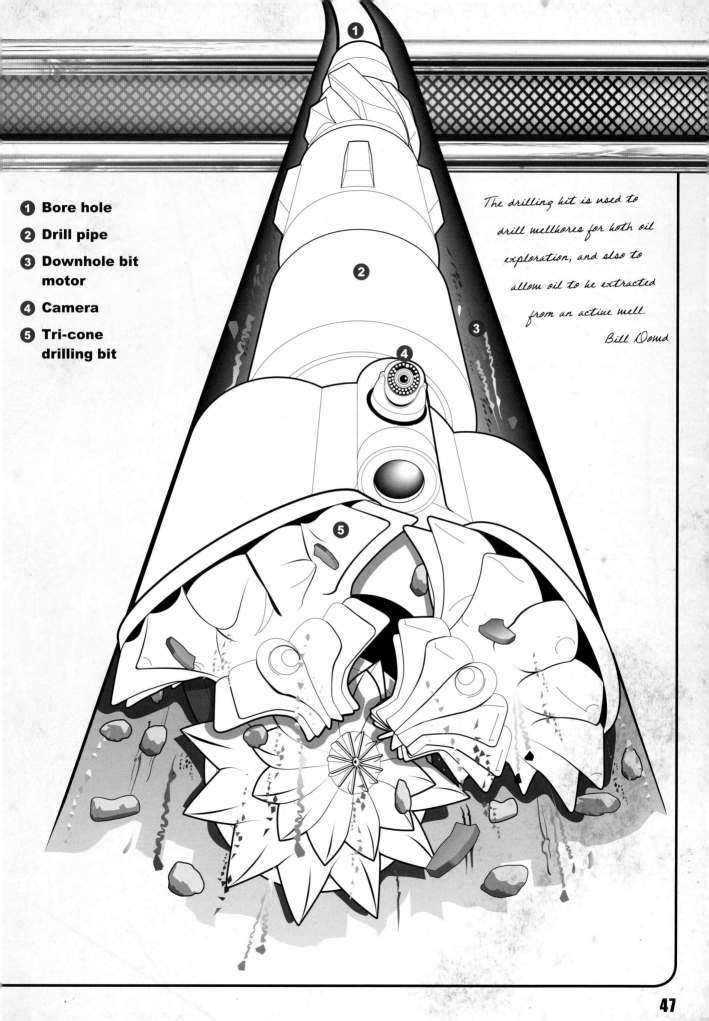

1 Bore hole
2 Drill pipe
3 Downhole bit motor
4 Camera
5 Tri-cone drilling bit

The drilling bit is used to drill wellbores for both oil exploration, and also to allow oil to be extracted from an active well.

Bill Dowd

Oil Haulers Wanted!

Do you have a Commercial Driver's License, and experience hauling oil, water, and sand? Terravex Energy needs qualified CDL drivers like you, and we need you now! We have hauler positions available in North Dakota, and can offer housing and health insurance as well as high pay. The minimum hiring requirements include:

- Class A CDL with 2 years' experience.
- Tanker and Hazmat endorsements.
- Clean background & driving record.
- Pass a pre-employment physical and drug test.

Join now, and receive a $2,000 sign-on bonus! If you aren't a CDL driver but possess an excellent driving record and other qualifications, Terravex has an employee-assistance program that will pay for your training to drive the heavy-duty trucks that make up the Terravex fleet.

Bill Dowd had never driven a big rig before, but that didn't stop him from "borrowing" one for a good cause

Tripp

1. Bumper
2. Peterbilt 'bird'
3. Grille
4. 6-cylinder turbo-diesel engine
5. Headlight
6. Parking light/turn signal
7. Engine compartment
8. Air horn
9. Cab lights
10. Windshield
11. Air cleaner
12. Rear-view mirror
13. Cabin
14. Vertical exhaust
15. Sleeper compartment

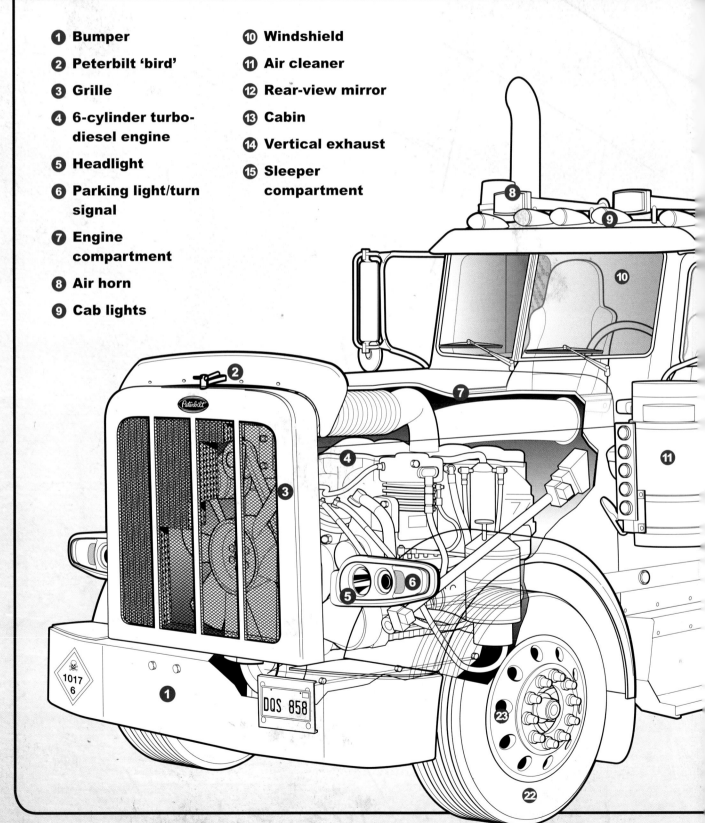

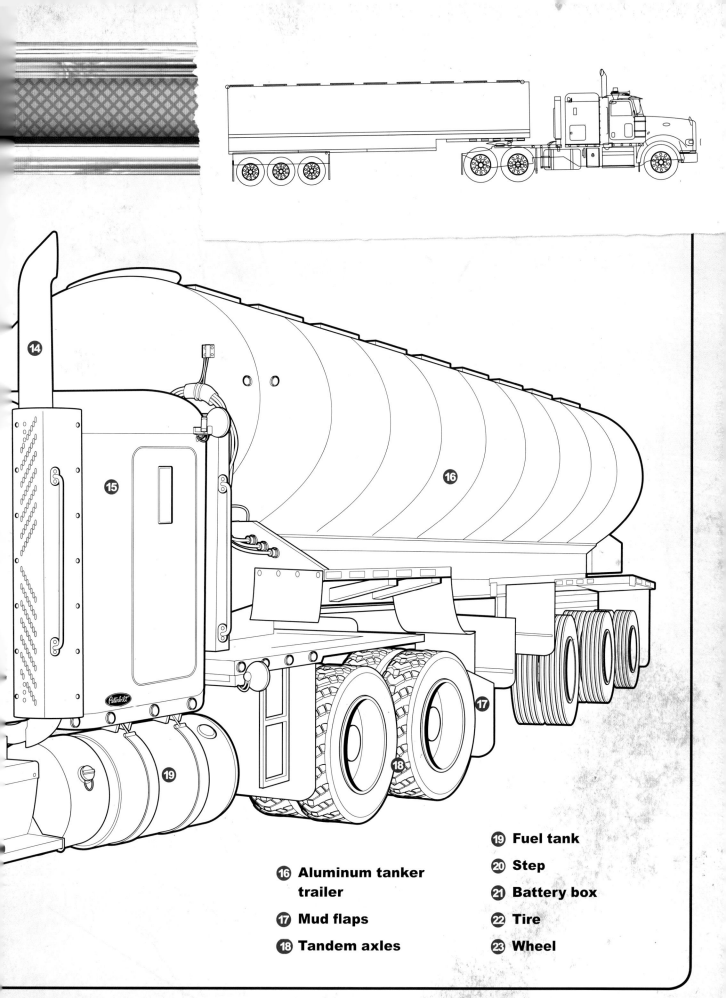

14

15

16

17

18

19

16 Aluminum tanker trailer

17 Mud flaps

18 Tandem axles

19 Fuel tank

20 Step

21 Battery box

22 Tire

23 Wheel

1. **Rotor blade**
2. **Rotor head**
3. **Communications aerial**
4. **NOTAR tail section**
5. **Vertical stabilizers**
6. **Tail boom**
7. **Engine exhaust**
8. **Twin PW207E turbine engines**
9. **Air intake**
10. **Passenger compartment**
11. **Landing skid**
12. **Crew compartment**
13. **Instrument panel**
14. **Instrument pitot tubes**

Reece Tenneson used the MD Explorer to shuttle between Terravex headquarters, drilling facilities, and Slowlin Field International Airport.

Bill Doud

Terravex Helicopter Seen Over Anderson

Terravex Energy executive Reece Tenneson arrived last night via a company helicopter at the drilling facility at Pankeska Rock. A recent press release from Terravex Energy suggests that the company anticipates that they'll collect more crude oil in the next quarter than they did in the past year.

The McDonnell Douglas Helicopters (MD) Explorer is used to transport Terravex Energy executives and other key personnel to Terravex operations throughout North Dakota. The MD 900 Explorer has eight seats (including the pilot), and has a range of 189 miles. The MD Explorer was the first McDonnell Douglas helicopter to use a NOTAR (an acronym derived from no tail rotor) anti-torque system, instead of a conventional tail rotor. The lack of a tail rotor increases safety and reduces external noise, reducing the impact of helicopter operations on local communities.

Biggest Truck in Anderson

Attention all truck-driving citizens of Sentinel County. If you thought you had the biggest set of wheels in the area, you can put that thought to rest. That's because the most enormous truck around belongs to Terravex Oil, a division of Terravex Energy.

The truck is a Liebherr T 282 C mining truck, which has the highest payload-to-empty-vehicle weight ratio in its class. Custom built for mining purposes, the Liebherr is strong, surprisingly lightweight, and extremely durable to endure the extreme conditions of mining operations. The vehicle combines a high-horsepower diesel engine with a Litronic Plus air-cooled circuits drive system that maximizes productivity and minimizes fuel consumption. Incredibly, the truck can haul 400 tons, and can reach nearly highway speeds.

The truck is equipped with a dynamic braking system that is virtually wear-free, resulting in fewer replacement parts. The T 282 C's air-cooled dry disc brakes do not require additional oil, pumps, filters, and cooling circuits. The drive system provides continuous acceleration and dynamic braking without shifting gears, and will automatically adjust the torque of the rear wheel motors. This feature maximizes traction and minimizes the wear to tires during low-speed handling. As for the truck's six tires, they measure 13.5-feet high, and each one costs $50,000.

The T 282 C's ergonomically designed operator cab offers functionality, visibility, and comfort to the driver, and complies with all operator seat vibration and noise exposure standards. The cab's 12-inch color touch-screen displays critical systems data, fault codes, and start-up sequences, all of which are constantly monitored by the Litronic Plus diagnostics system. If the operator door is open and the parking brake is not applied, visual and audible alarms are instantly activated.

TERRAVEX MINING TRUCK

1. Metal ladder
2. Radiator
3. Metal safety railings
4. Roof-mounted air conditioning unit
5. Rear-view mirror
6. Cab
7. Flexible rubber mud flaps
8. 400 ton (360 tonne) dump body
9. Welded-steel chassis frame
10. Two-stage lift hydraulics
11. Axle box
12. Front-wheel drive motor
13. Front-wheel disc brake
14. 3,500hp diesel engine

Believe it or not, the "Biggest Truck in Anderson" isn't the biggest on Earth. The BelAz 75710 can haul 50 tons more than the Liebherr T 282 C!

Tripp

TERRAVEX SECURITY

Immediately after the three creatures emerged from the Pankeska Rock site, Tenneson called in a man named Burke, a private security contractor. I don't know much about Burke. I'd never heard of him before, and couldn't find any official info about him, certainly nothing in Terravex company records. I do recall that Tenneson made an odd remark about Burke having been kicked out of the military for ethics violations or war crimes, something like that. I thought Tenneson was joking, but in hindsight, after seeing Burke in action and the way Tenneson dealt with him, it became obvious that Burke was no ordinary security guard.

Tenneson put Burke in charge of disposing of the two captured creatures, and also hunting down the one that escaped. Watching Burke and his team use electric cattle prods and Tasers to subdue the creatures, I felt sickened. At first, Tenneson professed that he didn't care one way or the other about how Burke got rid of the creatures, but I managed to persuade him to let me study the captured pair. I have no doubt that Burke would have killed the creatures without hesitation if Tenneson had given the order, so I was relieved that I at least stalled that possibility.

BILL DOWD

One of Mr. Weathers' security cameras recorded this image of Burke and his team entering Weathers' Garage. I guess it's obvious that Terravex wasn't very concerned about things like trespassing on private property.

Tripp

TERRAVEX SECURITY VEHICLES

The trucks used by Terravex's private security service are heavily modified Dodge Ram 3500 4x4 pickup trucks with diesel engines – essentially armored hot rods on steroids. I'll vouch for the fact that they went well over 100 miles per hour.

I think these trucks started off as 2006 model 3500s, the mega-cab versions. They're so heavily modified and covered by armor plating, it's tough to tell. The windows had bars over them, so they looked more like cages, and the headlights and tail lights were covered by protective metal too. Even the fender flares were heavy-duty stuff. The 2006 models probably started off with the 6.7L Cummins Turbo Diesel engine, the largest straight-six engines made for light-duty trucks, with Holset variable-geometry turbochargers, which were rated at 350 horsepower. But the way the Terravex trucks flew, I'm guessing someone may have dropped in Cummins' revamped 6.7L engines – the ones rated at 385 horsepower.

Burke's truck stood out from the other Dodge Rams because his had a higher suspension than the others, and also four big floodlights instead of the Bulldog Lighting LEDs that his staff had affixed to their armored bumpers. Burke's truck was also a dually (twin wheels on each side at the back) with extended fender flares, so it looked all-around larger and wider. Maybe that made him feel like top dog? Heck if I know. But best I can figure, Terravex didn't just have a fleet of security vehicles that could stop bullets, they had a fleet that looked like they were designed to catch bullets and spit them back.

And check out the wheels on these beasts. Burke's truck had XD Series Rock Stars – one-piece cast aluminum with the distinctive star on the center cap. His team had XD Series Misfits, one-piece cast aluminum ten-spoke wheels. I don't know whether these wheels were Burke's idea, but if they were, I'll say this much for him – he has good taste!

TRIPP

BURKE'S ARMORED DODGE RAM

1. **Reinforced heavy-duty bumper**
2. **Cooling fan**
3. **Off-road lighting**
4. **Headlight protectors**
5. **Bulletproof windshield**
6. **Bulletproof armor plating**
7. **Rock slider rail / step**
8. **Transfer gearbox**
9. **Front differential**
10. **Steering arm**

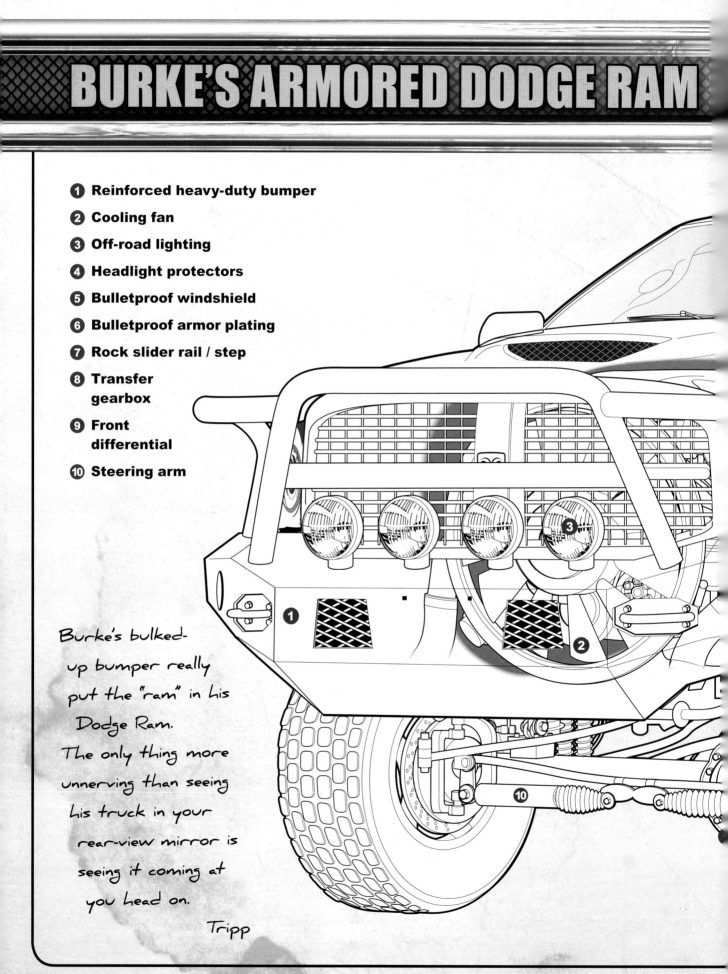

Burke's bulked-up bumper really put the "ram" in his Dodge Ram. The only thing more unnerving than seeing his truck in your rear-view mirror is seeing it coming at you head on.

Tripp

Dual rear tires enabled Burke's truck to carry heavy loads and haul large trailers, and also gave the truck better traction and stability.

THE CREATURES

I'd been working for Terravex Energy for fifteen years as a petroleum geologist before the incident at Pankeska Rock, and I was the lead scientist on that assignment. My job was to find oil for the company, but I was also paid to keep my mouth shut. If I found scientific evidence of anything that might put Terravex's investments at risk, my corporate supervisors would immediately and very strongly encourage me to find or fabricate data that supported their goals.

In other words, I was paid to lie when I had to. And, in case you're wondering, no, I'm not proud of that.

Although a plea bargain prevents me from making any public statements about Terravex while various state and federal agencies investigate the company, a few friends convinced me that it would be best to create a record of my final days with the company. Not necessarily best for me personally, but possibly best for the creatures that I unwittingly helped release to Earth's surface. It is my hope to convey to other scientists, who may at some future time encounter the creatures, that these remarkable, unusual life forms are highly intelligent and deserve our protection.

BILL DOWD

Explosion at the Terravex Oil Well

Smoke was still billowing from Terravex Energy's Pankeska Rock Drilling Facility this morning after a tremendous explosion tore through the facility last night. At least nine riggers were treated for minor injuries following the blast, which destroyed a large drilling rig, ancillary generators and other equipment, and at least one service vehicle.

According to a statement from Terravex executive Reece Tenneson, the explosion was "triggered by a drill penetrating an unexpected pocket of highly pressurized gas, causing a blow-out – an uncontrolled rush of gas to the surface." Tenneson stressed that a "very small amount of gas" was released, and he commended Terravex Oil workers for "their professionalism and courage, for preventing what could have been a deadly accident."

Rigger Wade Coley was on the scene when the accident happened. Briefly interviewed by the Sentinel's TV news affiliate, Coley said, "I heard an explosion and the tower [derrick] crashed. Guys were running and shouting. That's all I'm really allowed to say."

The Sentinel has requested specific details about the incident, such as whether the oil rig's blow-out preventer had been properly functioning at the time of the explosion. So far, the only response from Tenneson's office is an automated message that claims "the accident is being thoroughly investigated."

Terravex's statement about the gas leak was a lie spun by Tenneson. What really happened...

I'd pinpointed the location of what appeared to be a large pocket of water – two miles below the Earth's surface – between our drill and the petroleum reserve that we'd been aiming for. Although I was keenly aware that discovering water at that level is important scientifically, since the existence of water might indicate the presence of an ecosystem, I also knew that the pressure at that depth is well over 10,000psi. Moreover, I knew that the water would be supersaturated with nitrogen, so I was certain that the water wouldn't have any nutrients to support life. Therefore I authorized our drill team to punch through rock and into the water pocket. The drill was equipped with a camera, and when the creatures swam into view, I was stunned. Then a technician informed me that the bore into the water pocket had destabilized the well, and the pressure rose faster than the blow-out preventers could handle it. That's what caused the explosion, and sent three creatures straight to the surface.

BILL DOWD

The day after an accident at Pankeska Rock, Mr. Weathers went out to the drilling site and returned to his scrap yard with a wrecked Terravex truck, the one that had the 6.4 liter Hemi V8 that he said I could have. Later, I told Meredith about the wreck, and she figured out that Creatch must have hidden inside it, and escaped from Pankeska Rock.

Tripp

Reece Tenneson called in a security contractor named Burke, to subdue the creatures. Burke's team captured two creatures (that turned out to be Creatch's parents) and forced them into waste-water storage containers, but a third creature escaped. Tenneson's immediate solution to avoid any problems was to destroy the captured creatures, but I managed to discourage that idea.

Tenneson made arrangements for me to use a Terravex warehouse to study the two creatures. Although both creatures had exhibited incredible strength after their explosive expulsion from the oil well, within twenty-four hours, I noted that they

appeared to be increasingly weak and subdued. They may have endured their journey up and out of the well without significant injuries, but Burke and his team had used Tasers and blunt weapons on the creatures, so I had no doubt that they'd been injured. But unfortunately, I didn't know how to treat them. Not for the first time in my life, I regretted that I wasn't a biologist.

Looking at the creatures, I easily observed that one was larger than the other, and for some reason I began to assume that the larger creature was a male, and the smaller one was female. Because of their tentacles, to me they resembled octopus or squid, which prompted some hasty research on cephalopods. I learned that the creatures were unlike any cephalopods on record. And as I watched their skin become less taut, and more worn and wrinkled-looking, I could only assume that they were dying.

I tried feeding them molds, fungi, bacteria cultures, and nematodes, among other things. As I mused that they must eat *something* in their habitat under the oil beds, it suddenly occurred to me: oil. A cabinet in the warehouse contained automotive supplies, including a jug of motor oil. I brought the jug to the larger creature, and he drank from it eagerly. For a moment, I thought he'd drink it all, but he extended the jug to the female, and she drank the oil too.

While watching them, I rubbed my chin. The only reason I remember that was because the male made eye contact with me, shifted one of his tentacles below his mouth, and began mimicking me. As I already noted, I'm a geologist, not a biologist. But how could I not ascertain that the creatures possessed intelligence and empathy?

BILL DOWD

ANATOMICAL OBSERVATIONS

Although I never determined that the two captured creatures were indeed male and female, I did note various physical similarities and differences. Like octopuses, both have eight flexible arms, which they use for grasping as well as for propulsion. But unlike cephalopods, the creatures don't have beaks. Instead, they have mouths with teeth. They can breathe both on land and underwater, and they also have blow-holes that release excess oil, water, and debris.

From my observations, I believe the creatures possess a hive intelligence. Even when they couldn't see each other directly, one knew what the other knew almost instantly. In that capacity, their minds may be similar to ants or bees, although I believe they're much more intelligent than ordinary insects.

As for their petroleum diet, the best that I could determine was that they metabolize oil like the bacteria *Alcanivorax borkumensis*, and that their anatomy works like internal combustion engines. The oil literally gives them energy, and also seems to enable them to generate electricity. I wish I'd had more time to study them further.

BILL DOWD

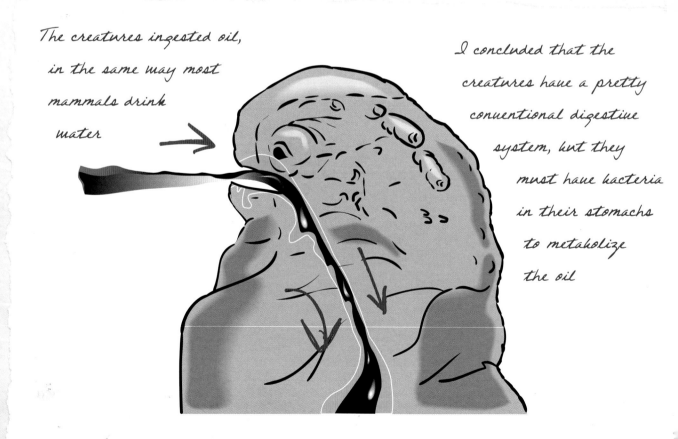

The creatures ingested oil, in the same way most mammals drink water

I concluded that the creatures have a pretty conventional digestive system, but they must have bacteria in their stomachs to metabolize the oil

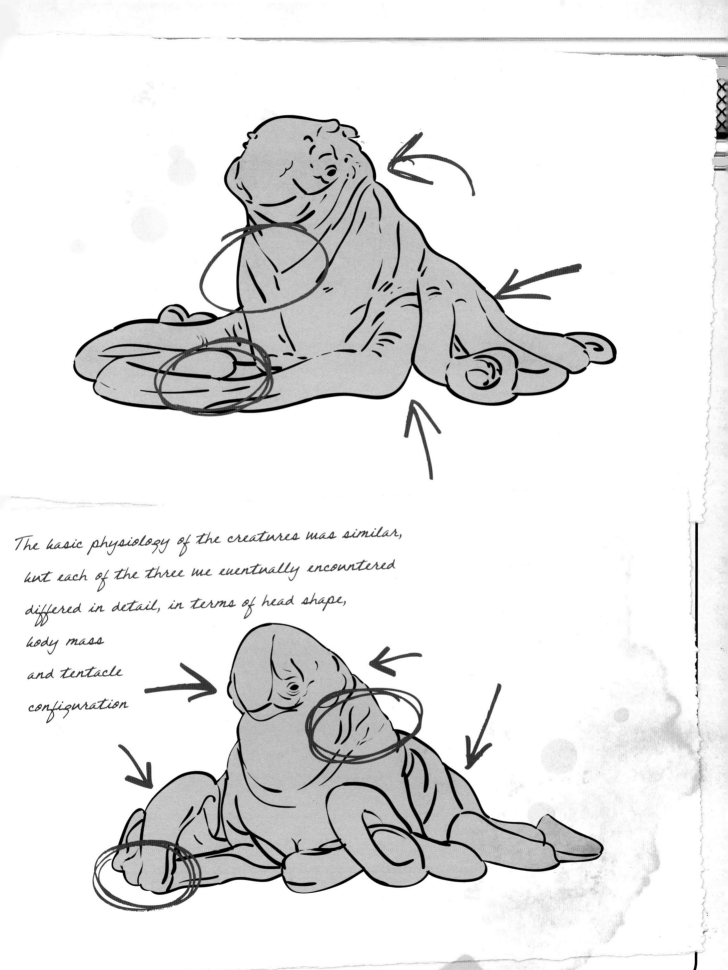

The basic physiology of the creatures was similar, but each of the three we eventually encountered differed in detail, in terms of head shape, body mass and tentacle configuration

JUNKYARD FIGHT

Transcript from Central Dispatch, Sentinel County Sheriff's Department

Dispatcher: Sheriff's department, how can I help you?

Tripp: My name's Tripp Coley, and I'm at Weathers' Garage off 112, and there's a wild animal in here.

Dispatcher: Are you injured?

Tripp: No, but you gotta send someone out here. This thing is really big.

Dispatcher: Is it a bear?

Tripp: I don't know what it is. I've never seen anything like it.

Dispatcher: Are you in danger right now?

Tripp: Why do you think I called you?! You think I would have called if I thought everything here was fine? It's throwing stuff around and nearly killed me!

Dispatcher: Where are you right now? Can the animal get to you?

Tripp: No, I mean... I don't think so. I got it locked up, but it's thrashing around. I'm going to check on it.

Dispatcher: Locked up where? Hello? Hello?

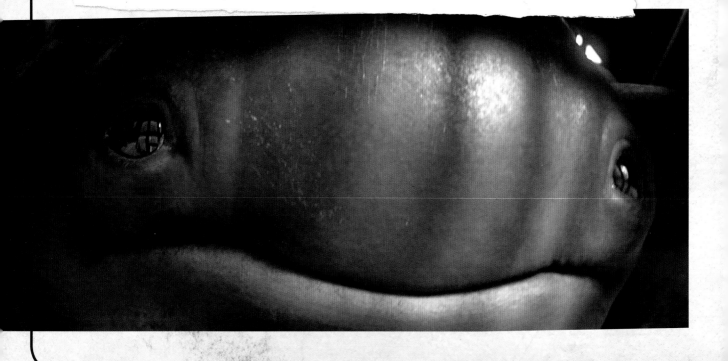

72

STRANGE TRESPASSER

It's hard for me to describe my first encounter with Creatch. I remember feeling the mental rush, the excitement of the moment. I'd never felt so alert, angry, afraid, curious, and confused, and all at the same time.

Anyway, here's how I remember it.

I was inside Weathers' Garage, working on a truck. Mr. Weathers had gone for the night, and he'd left his dog, Hulk, chained up outside. Hulk and I were the only ones around, or so I thought. I'd turned the TV on, just for something to listen to, when I heard

my father's name mentioned on the news. That's how I learned where he was, that he was working as a rigger for Terravex at the Pankeska Rock site, and that he'd been there when the explosion happened.

But then I heard some noises from outside, a strange growl followed by a loud crash. Hulk started barking, and I turned off the TV, grabbed a crowbar, and went outside. I found Hulk cowering on the end of his chain, spooked. I noticed the shelves holding motor oil had been knocked over, and that all the oil cartons were emptied and crushed, as if they'd been sucked dry. The hard plastic gasoline cans were crushed the same way.

It was dark inside the garage, but I saw something move, and I swung the crowbar at it. The impact sounded squishy. Next thing I knew, the thing – whatever it was – was coming after me. I tried hiding in the mechanic's pit, but then a tentacle dipped down into the pit, and I knew I was dealing with a creature. Creatch slithered into the pit, and I managed to scramble out and temporarily trapped him.

I called in the cavalry, but when Sheriff Rick arrived with his deputies, Creatch had vanished, making Rick think I was either a liar or crazy. After the cops left, I realized Creatch must have escaped through a small hole in one of the doors covering the pit. I was furious. Creatch definitely won the first round!

TRIPP

I'm used to improvising and working out how to deal with unfamiliar machinery, but an encounter with a strange creature was a whole new experience!

STRANGE TRESPASSER

The day after my first encounter with Creatch, I went to school, and did my best to behave like nothing had happened at Weathers' Garage.

After school, I went back to the garage, and was working on my truck when I heard a weird growl that made me realize Creatch hadn't run off. I decided to try to kill him so everyone would know I wasn't lying! I set a trap by placing a full oil barrel on the bed of the car compactor, and leaving a trail of oil across the garage floor. Then I hid in the shadows and waited. Pretty soon, Creatch slithered out from his own hiding spot and – just as I predicted – pulled his way up onto the crusher.

But watching Creatch, seeing his eyes, the way he moved... somehow, I knew that he wasn't just hungry and smart, but also that he was scared. Then he looked straight at me, which surprised me, and I accidentally activated the crusher. I was able to pull Creatch free before the crushing plate slammed into the bed.

TRIPP

SUPERCREATURE STRENGTH

It wasn't until after I'd rescued Creatch that I realized just how strong he was. We were still at Weathers' Garage, and Creatch saw the damaged Terravex truck that had been brought in from the Pankeska drilling site. I don't know whether Creatch recognized that particular truck, or the Terravex logo, but seeing the truck definitely made him angry. He reached out with his tentacles to grab wrenches, crowbars, even empty oil drums, and then flung the stuff at the Terravex truck.

But it wasn't until Creatch picked up a heavy engine block and hurled it at the truck that I knew he was more powerful than anything I'd ever seen. Years back, watching a TV show about animals, I saw an elephant lifting logs and a grizzly bear tearing up a garbage bin, but I doubt those animals could pick up an engine block and throw it like Creatch did.

TRIPP

Scientific Observations

Because the creatures evolved deep below the Earth's surface, and thrive under extreme pressures, it's not surprising that they're remarkably strong. Although they move somewhat awkwardly outside their natural habitat (that is, when their movements are unassisted by technology), they are still capable of lifting and moving heavy objects with apparent ease. However, the creatures require considerable amounts of oil to maintain their strength. When deprived of oil for more than 24 hours, they become discernibly weaker. I don't know how long they can survive without oil, but the ingestion of oil seems to dramatically reenergize them, possibly restoring their full strength in less than an hour.

Bill Dowd

MONSTER MODIFICATIONS

According to Tripp, if he hadn't seen Creatch slither onto a small trailer in Weathers' Garage and propel the trailer across the ground, he never would have imagined trying to use Creatch as an engine for a truck.

Now that I think of it, it's fortunate that Tripp and Creatch met when and where they did, and that Tripp knows so much about cars and trucks. If Creatch had appeared anywhere else in Sentinel County, people probably would have just phoned the police or tried to kill Creatch themselves.

As for me, I didn't know how useful I could be when Tripp told me he wanted to modify his truck to better accommodate Creatch. And later, when he decided we needed *more* trucks... but I'm getting ahead of myself. Considering I knew practically nothing about trucks, I'm glad I could help at all!

MEREDITH

I've already mentioned how Creatch could crush oil drums and lift heavy stuff, but it wasn't until Meredith and I were making our getaway from Burke's team that I knew Creatch was *really* powerful. I mean, Creatch wheeling around on a flatbed trailer was one thing, but getting my old Dodge truck to tear off and leave a trail of dust, that was another thing entirely.

The original Dodge C-Series light-duty pickup came with either a standard 120-horsepower Flathead straight-six engine or an optional 145-horsepower Power-Dome V8. I know what those engines can do, but I also know what a 1,300-horsepower hot rod sounds like and how fast those machines can cover ground. The way we raced off, I believe we could have given those hot rods some serious competition.

But I had practically no control over Creatch. I struggled with the wheel, tapped the gas, and pumped the brakes, or rather I *tried* to struggle with those things. For all practical purposes, Creatch had possessed my truck, and he wasn't in any mood for learning the subtleties of mechanical engineering. Like me, he probably mostly just wanted to get away from Burke.

Creatch veered into the woods, somehow managed to avoid hitting any especially large trees, and then down a hill before slowing to a stop. The inside of the truck had gotten incredibly warm, and I suspected Creatch was overheating. Meredith and I got out, and I finally had the chance to show her what was under the hood. I was afraid she'd totally freak out, but she held herself together and seemed more worried about Creatch and what would happen to him than anything else. All I could think was that I no longer needed to drop a 6.4 liter Hemi V8 engine into my truck. Instead, my truck would be Creatch-powered.

TRIPP

Creatch seemed to be able to generate electricity through his body, maybe from the oil he drank. I'm no scientist, but I guess it must work a little like an electric eel.

Creatch somehow used his tentacles to turn the truck's driveshafts. He made V8 torque look puny!

INTUITIVE MECHANIC

After we got away from the Terravex security team at Weathers' Garage, Meredith let me bring Creatch to her family's farm, which has a large barn.

The barn was loaded with tools, scrap metal, tractor parts, and other stuff, and Meredith said I could borrow some things so I could make adjustments to the Old Mutt. My goal was to increase space in the engine compartment so Creatch would have more room to move and breathe. I also wanted to figure out how he had worked the axles and tires for power and steering. Mostly, I was hoping to figure out how to control him, make him more obedient. Big mistake, but I'll get to that later.

I opened the hood and looked under the truck, and I saw how Creatch's tentacles wrapped around various parts of the truck. When I placed a few broad bands of scrap metal under the truck, and motioned him to move aside to let me work, he seemed to immediately understand that I was trying to make the engine compartment more comfortable for him. He was watching for only a minute or so while I used a screwdriver to secure some metal bits into place when he grabbed a spare screwdriver and began helping me. The way he used the screwdriver was wild. He could make it spin as fast as a power drill!

I don't think he understood everything I said, but I was talking while I worked, just kind of thinking out loud about the driveshaft and differential gears, and what I needed to do so Creatch could operate them better. So I was surprised when his tentacles began feeling out the parts of the truck that I'd been talking about. He was definitely learning his way around my truck.

His strength came in handy too, when I needed to elevate the truck to work on the tires. Who needs a jack when you have a creature that can lift the truck for you?

TRIPP

Even though I'm comfortable working with power tools, carving up an old truck so it could house and be powered by a creature was unlike anything I'd ever done before. Not just because of Creatch, but because the work was entirely improvised. It's not like you can just buy a book about how to modify and rig a vehicle for a creature, though I guess that's partly what I've done with this book. Like I said earlier though, this book was Meredith's idea.

Anyway, I had to do some serious improvising, and I had to do it fast. I wanted to make sure that Creatch would fit under the hood and operate the wheels, and that the modified truck wouldn't fall apart, and I was also concerned about getting off Meredith's property before anyone from Terravex tracked me down. Fortunately, I'd learned a lot about improvising at Mr. Weathers' shop, where the age and condition of a car, as well as the customer's budget, sometimes determined whether it was best to modify or fabricate some needed part.

With Creatch helping me however he could, I worked on modifying the Old Mutt all night in Meredith's barn. I cut lengths of scrap metal to create supports below the engine compartment, so Creatch could rest more easily on his stomach, and still be able to extend his tentacles to different areas of the car. I guess the supports could be called "belly bands." Working up close with Creatch gave me a better idea of how he functioned as an engine. His tentacles had these little hairlike things, like cilia. I know when Meredith reads this, she'll probably say, "You didn't even know about cilia before I became your tutor." That would be true. Anyway, from what I observed, Creatch's cilia generated massive torque on the axles, so I gave him more surface area to grip, and not just at the differential, but at each tire!

TRIPP

This diagram gives you a good idea of how Creatch first fitted inside my slightly modified Dodge C-Series truck. I smoothed down various odd bits of metal to make Creatch more comfortable. I was afraid Creatch might slide around a bit under the hood, or that a piece of metal might jab or cut him, but either his tentacles kept him from sliding about, or the shape of his body kept him in place.

I reworked the grille so Creatch could see more clearly through it, but only when I wanted him to. I fabricated metal strips that stretched horizontally across the inside of the grille, and rigged the strips with some levers so they could be opened and closed like blinds. I figured that was a good way to control him, to prevent him from taking off in any direction. I connected the truck's throttle wire to the levers, so all I had to do was push the gas pedal to open the blinds. Pressing the brake released the wire to close the blinds. It was kind of tricky, but hey, it worked.

The blinds would also help conceal Creatch if I ever parked my truck in a public area. Yeah, I know, very selfish of me, but at the time, all I could think was that I could use Creatch as my ticket out of Anderson.

When I was done, Creatch and I were both eager for a test drive.

TRIPP

The poor little guy looks kinda cramped in there, doesn't he? Don't worry, I made more room for him.

I got under the hood so I could see what visibility Creatch had, and realized I needed to improve that area too.

Tripp

1. Front bumper
2. Grille bars
3. Creatch support frame
4. Windshield
5. Windshield visor
6. Load compartment
7. Rear fender extension
8. Rear bumper
9. Rock slider rail/step
10. Front suspension
11. Road tires
12. Headlamp

Okay, I admit, the test drive didn't start off very well.

The problem was that I started off thinking that I could 'control' Creatch. He didn't like that one bit. We were conducting our test in the wheat fields and hills around Meredith's farm, where no one could see us. As soon as he figured out that I was the one operating the blinders across the grille, that it was entirely up to me whether he could see anything, he started bucking around. He somehow jostled the driver's door open and tossed me out. Stupid me for not wearing a seatbelt.

But I was even more stupid because I hadn't considered Creatch's perspective, his take on the whole situation. I mean, why should he allow me to decide whether he should go fast or stop? What was in it for him? I forgot how smart he was. I couldn't treat him like a pet. I had to treat him with respect.

While Creatch and I were trying to sort out our relationship inside the truck, Meredith got her horse out of the barn and started riding alongside us. At first, I thought she and the horse would just distract Creatch, but I realized pretty fast that she was helping Creatch figure out the basics of going slow, going faster, coming to a stop, turning, and backing up. And I guess she was helping me too, which I appreciated. I know a lot about cars and trucks, but Meredith's smart about a lot of other things.

Creatch was a fast learner, and adventurous too, eager to find out what he could do with his truck 'body'. When Meredith guided her horse to jump over a log, Creatch hesitated for a moment, but then he figured out how to jump too. And man, what a bounce. Made me realize that larger tires would be useful.

Afterward, Meredith's horse started galloping faster, and I could sense that Creatch wanted to test his own speed. We let loose over the hills. It was fantastic!

The experience also showed me that I needed to make a few more modifications to the truck.

TRIPP

SECOND ALTERATION

After the test drive, Creatch and I brought the truck back to Meredith's barn. Although we literally made a few wrong turns, I'd gotten a better understanding of how Creatch controlled the wheels, and also how I could make some adjustments so both of us could handle the truck better. Another thing that was painfully obvious was that parts of Creatch's body were exposed, so I'd have to make some modifications to help conceal him. Even though his tentacles weirdly blended in with the machinery, the fact that they were at all visible made me want to cover them

up. I hoped that would discourage even a casual inspection, especially if we encountered the Terravex security team again.

To better conceal Creatch, I needed to give him more room under the hood. I expanded the mostly empty engine compartment by cutting away parts of the hood, and then I bulked it up with more scrap metal. I also built oversized fender flares, extending them up and away from the wheel wells to give Creatch more room. I didn't bother to paint the fender flares because I thought the bare metal and welds made the truck look even more awesome, more muscular.

Even though I'd reinforced the belly bands, and was confident that Creatch could move more freely, I wanted the truck to be more elevated to prevent Creatch's tentacles from scraping on the ground, and also help him jump if he had to. Larger tires were just what we needed. Meredith's father had a bunch of old tractor tires lying around, and I was amazed to find a set of Interco Super Swamper tires in a pile, covered with dust. These particular tires weren't just made for off-road vehicles, but for rock-crawling competitions. I have no idea why her father bought the tires, but I wasn't about to let them languish when I could put them to good use.

The end result of all this work? A truly monstrous monster truck.

TRIPP

In the diagram here, you can see how the bulked-up hood gives Creatch more room to move. You can also see that I removed the thick horizontal bars from the old grille, and replaced them with a row of thin vertical bars that I fabricated. The new grille gives Creatch better visibility, and also makes the truck look like it's gnashing a set of metal teeth!

Even though during the test drive I'd become aware that Creatch seemed to have some way of holding himself in position under the truck, I tweaked the engine's support frame so it would better accommodate Creatch. I realized I had to stop thinking of the engine compartment as – well, an engine compartment! I needed to keep in mind that Creatch was alive, that he need a customized cockpit. Also, I was warming up to the idea that Creatch wasn't merely a living "replacement" engine, but that we might be able to work together to drive the truck like co-pilots.

I also wanted to make sure Creatch could keep cool. The new grille definitely allowed for more air flow, but I also placed cooling ducts on the rear fender flares for more circulation. All the fender flares and extensions served a dual purpose, giving Creatch more room while also concealing his tentacles.

After I finished the second alteration, I couldn't help wondering how the original Dodge C-Series designers and engineers might have reacted if they could have seen my handiwork. I'm guessing they would have been mortified!

TRIPP

Gotta love the metal "teeth." The truck looks like it's snarling!

Lucky for me, Meredith's father's tools included a rivet gun along with plenty of rivets, perfect for fabricating the truck's metal coverings.

Tripp

1. Front nudge bar
2. Open grille
3. Hood strap
4. Creatch support frame
5. Windshield
6. Windshield visor
7. Twin spare wheels
8. Flared rear fender
9. Cooling duct
10. Rock slider rail/step
11. Front fender extension
12. Off-road tire

Jake goes to Montgomery High School, and I was never friends with him. So far as I know, he's always been a jerk. But I admit I used to kind of envy his truck, and not just because it was entirely wasted on him.

The RAM 2500 Power Wagon is a high-performance pickup and a dang impressive machine. Like the RAM 2500, it's a genuine workhorse, but instead of a 5.7-liter V8, it has a 6.4-liter Hemi V8, an even more powerful muscle-car engine, the same kind used for the Dodge Charger SRT8. The engine produces 410 horsepower and 429lb ft of torque, and it can tow over 10,000 pounds. All that power, combined with 33-inch tires, a ground clearance of 14.5 inches, and an innovative "Articulink" suspension, adds up to a truck with definite off-road capabilities. The Articulink suspension incorporates high-movement joints at the control-arm-to-axle mount, which allows for remarkable flexibility and axle articulation.

Sounds awesome, right? But Jake never did much more with it than commute to school and the shopping center, probably because he didn't want to scuff up the custom paint job. Like I said... a waste of machinery.

Fortunately, Jake wasn't quite as loaded as I thought he was, or he and his family were flat-out lazy about making payments on his flashy green toy. Either way, circumstances eventually led to me and my friends putting the Power Wagon to good use.

TRIPP

When Meredith and I stopped at a gas station to feed Creatch, Jake tried to impress us by gunning his truck's engine.

I wish Meredith had take a picture of Jake's face when he heard Creatch respond with a growl that almost blasted out the Power Wagon's windows!

Trip

I've already mentioned that Meredith was the one who connected the dots to figure out that Creatch came from the Pankeska Rock drilling site. She also told me she's an activist for Youth for Animal Rights, and she was really concerned for Creatch's life. I was less concerned about Creatch's well-being than I was into the idea of showing off my creature-powered truck to my father. I just wanted to impress him. That's all.

I found out that my father was staying at a temporary camp in Clearview, and Meredith insisted on going with me and Creatch. She thought if we talked with Terravex workers, they might fill us in on the accident at Pankeska Rock, so we could find out more about Creatch.

Big mistake all around. Not only wasn't my father glad to see me at the camp, he actually snuck off and called Terravex security on us! Thanks to Creatch's fast thinking, Meredith and I escaped and hid out at her family's hunting cabin.

But the next morning, Creatch was gone. Along with my truck. I never imagined he'd just take off like that.

TRIPP

That's me meeting Tripp's father, Wade Coley, for the first time. I don't know the details about how and why Tripp's parents split up, and it's really none of my business, but for what it's worth... I hope Tripp appreciates that he was raised by his mother.

Meredith

I agree... my mom's terrific. She knows. I told her.

Tripp

That truck chase through Anderson was like the ultimate fairground ride! I was trying to shake off those Terravex goons, but I never could have pulled off some of those crazy moves without Creatch. It was a great piece of teamwork, but not something I'd want to do every day. I'm not sure Meredith enjoyed it as much as I did...

Tripp

Monster Truck Mayhem

Video captured by several pedestrians and a motorist corroborated accounts from more than a dozen other people who claimed sightings of what all described as a "monster truck" on extremely large tires, which destroyed property and caused at least three minor accidents in downtown Anderson. The video also appears to substantiate claims that the truck had two teenagers on board.

"I was standing just stepping out of the library when I saw the truck," said library director Tom O'Donnell, "and even though it was going fast, from where I stood, I had a clear view through the windows. There was a young guy in the driver's seat and a girl passenger. The driver was crazy, but he sure knew how to handle the truck, though he was barely staying in control – he was driving like a monster!" Asked if he noticed the license plates, O'Donnell said, "You're kidding – I'm not sure it had any, but it was going way too fast for me to be sure, and I was concentrating on keeping out of the way."

Another eyewitness, who asked to remain anonymous, said she had noticed a Terravex Energy truck pass by when she "saw the monster truck just a few seconds later. We already have enough trouble in Anderson with all those oil trucks tearing our roads, but now, with these oil-rich kids racing around in their gas-guzzling big-wheel toys, it's getting so I don't like going out any more."

Calls to the Sentinel County Sheriff's Office confirmed that no large-wheeled off-road vehicles have been reported missing, and that Sheriff Rick Lovick and his deputies are aware of the reports about the damaged property and are investigating.

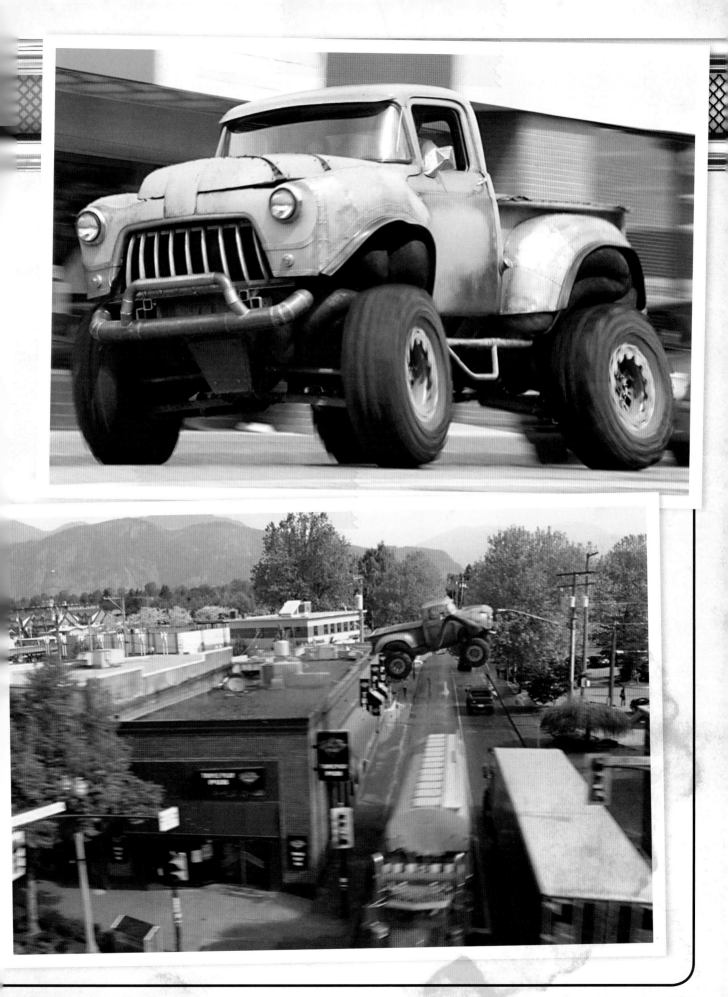

WAREHOUSE BREAKOUT

Burke and his men captured Creatch, along with my truck, at the Terravex oil depot. Meredith and I showed up just in time for them to nab us too. They hauled us in to meet a Terravex hot-shot, Reece Tenneson, who essentially did his best to let us know that all the power and money was on his side, and that if we didn't agree to a payoff, he'd make things very hard for us.

Meredith and I also realized that Tenneson was planning on getting rid of the creatures even if we didn't accept his terms. So I made like I was reasonable because I figured that was our best chance of living to fight another day, and believe me, I was looking for a fight.

Fortunately, the meeting also gave us Bill Dowd – an ally, even though he was a reluctant ally at first. Bill wanted us to contact the government. But I proposed another idea – that he should do whatever he could to get the creatures out of the oil depot.

And you know what? He did just that.

TRIPP

Reece Tenneson offered us land leases and security for our families if we played ball with him, and forgot all about the creatures.

What a piece of slime.

Meredith

Tenneson had already scheduled a Terranex truck to remove the creatures from the warehouse and transport them along with a waste shipment that was destined for the deep-injection wells, so there wouldn't be any trace of them. I couldn't let that happen. I'd never driven such a big truck before. Or stolen anything from Terranex. Or rescued incredibly rare life forms. I guess this picture shows that I was kind of excited at the time.

Bill Dowd

REPO MEN

After Bill Dowd agreed to get the creatures out of the Terravex warehouse, I realized that transporting the creatures in one large truck wasn't an option. I needed to modify two more trucks, and fast.

Mr. Weathers was more than willing to help out. I asked him if he had any suitable trucks on his repo list. Surprise, surprise, it turned out that Jake had fallen behind on payments for his Power Wagon. So Meredith and I went with Mr. Weathers over to Jake's house, where we found the Power Wagon parked out front. Mr. Weathers' tow truck is not the quietest vehicle on the planet, but we had some good luck in that Jake – who was inside his house at the time –

was preoccupied with an extremely loud video game.

Once the Power Wagon was locked onto the tow truck, Mr. Weathers, Meredith and I took off. Unfortunately, the Power Wagon was the only truck on the list that was usable for a creature. I told Mr. Weathers my plan, which required another truck, that we had to lift the engine, raise the suspension, cut up the body, and customize the axles and manifold. Mr. Weathers pointed out that he didn't have the tools or parts to modify two trucks overnight.

That's when I decided to call in a favor from Sam Geldon.

TRIPP

Sam: who r u?

Tripp: hey sam its me tripp

Sam: tripp coley?

Tripp: yeah i need a favor

Sam: is this a joke?

Tripp: huh?

Sam: howd u get my #?

Tripp: from meredith

Sam: Meredith?

Tripp: yeah

Sam: o howd SHE get my #?

Tripp: yearbook i think

Sam: i cant believe ur texting me dude thats so cool!

Tripp: cool yeah cool i really need a favor

Sam: 4 u? name it!!!

Tripp: u have keys 4 ur dads dealership?

Sam: dealership like u mean his business?

Tripp: yeah

Sam: no keys but i know the keycode but...

Tripp: can u get me in?

Sam: tripp sorry i want 2 help but i gotta ask y???

Tripp: i need tools 2 work on some trucks

Sam: sorry dude i cant let u steal tools

Tripp: huh?

Sam: i cant help u steal from my dad

Tripp: NO STEALING i just need to use his shop and tools

Sam: y?

Tripp: 2 work on some trucks

Sam: stolen?

Tripp: NO!

Sam: what kind of work?

Tripp: major surgery

Sam: COOL!!! but u wont take or break anything?

Tripp: promise

Sam: ok but i hope ur not joking

Tripp: totally serious how soon can u b there?

Sam: 20 minutes?

Tripp: make it 15

Sam: ok but this work is it legal?

Tripp: not exactly

Sam: COOL!!!

BUILD TEAM

As soon as Sam Geldon agreed to let me do some work in his dad's dealership, I called Bill, and told him where to bring the creatures. When Mr. Weathers, Meredith and I showed up at the Dodge dealership, Sam was already waiting for us. I thought he might be alarmed when I told him what we intended to do to the confiscated Power Wagon, and that he'd totally freak when I told him I needed to modify an additional truck. But Sam was beyond eager to help. I could hardly believe it when he offered up a brand new Dodge Ram Rebel.

Sam also jumped right in to help with the modifications. Even though we were in the same auto-shop class, I had no idea he was so good with tools, that he wasn't at all squeamish about cutting metal. Mr. Weathers had brought along various parts, including most of a salvaged suspension system for the Power Wagon, but Sam didn't hesitate to kick in everything else we needed.

As for Meredith, she didn't sit around waiting for anyone to invite her to join the build team. She just said, "Put me to work," and the four of us worked through the night. Here are a few pics that we took.

TRIPP

Even though Sam owed me a favor, I knew that I was probably overdoing it when I asked for a truck. If I didn't know better, I'd swear he'd been just itching to carve up a brand new Rebel, and turn it into a monster.

Tripp

My pleasure, Tripp! Just don't let my dad see this book!

Sam

BUILD COMPLETE!

It would take a long time to describe everything we did to the Power Wagon and the Rebel, but here's a few items you may find interesting. The Power Wagon started off with Fuel Deep Lip Dune wheels, which have a machined black finish, and Interco tires. We replaced those with larger wheels and Mickey Thompson Baja Claw tires. We also installed a PSC Motorsports Trail Series 2.5-inch Double End Steering Cylinder Kit and a spring-over-axle suspension system. For the Rebel, we pretty much did the same thing, lifting the suspension to increase ground clearance.

Obviously, we also beefed up both trucks with a lot of accessories to help conceal the creatures. I'm glad we took a few pics because we didn't have much time to admire our work. As soon as Bill Dowd arrived with the three creatures, we had to help them into the trucks, and prepare to leave before Burke's crew tracked us down. When we released the three creatures from the shipping containers, it became clear that they were family, that the two larger creatures were the parents of Creatch, who'd powered my truck.

Oh, I forgot to mention that we removed the engines from both the Power Wagon and the Rebel to accommodate the father and mother creature. We left the engines intact, which I think Sam appreciated. It's not as if we left nothing behind at the Dodge dealership. We left Sam there too, but only because he was sound asleep, and we didn't want to disturb him.

TRIPP

Even though Creatch had been stuck on his own inside a shipping container, he still seemed to have a smile for me! You gotta admire that.
Tripp

MODIFIED POWER WAGON

JAKE WOULD STRUGGLE TO RECOGNIZE HIS POWER WAGON
AFTER WE COMPLETED OUR HANDIWORK

The sculpted hood is appropriately shaped for the father creature's above-ground transport.

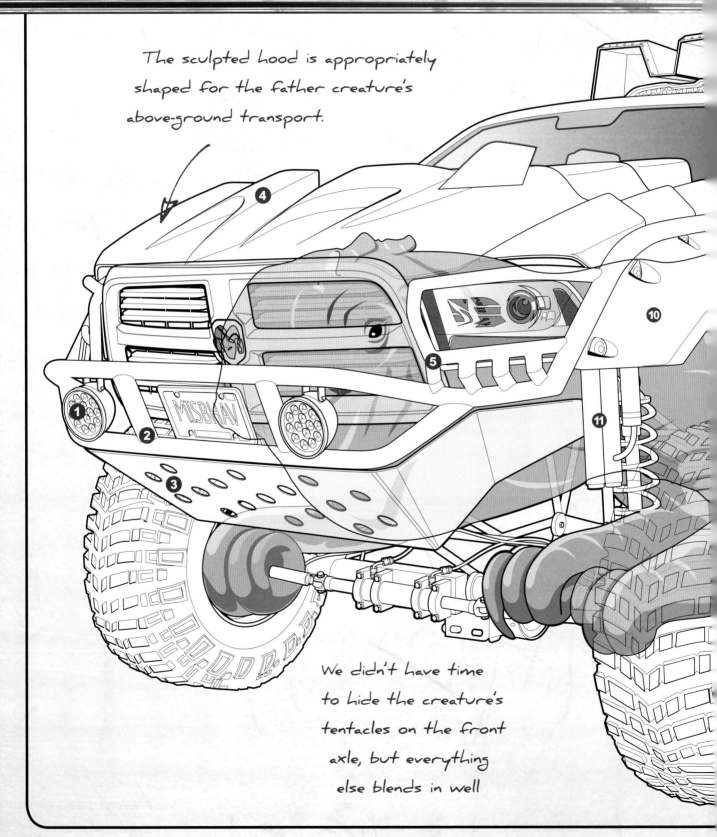

We didn't have time to hide the creature's tentacles on the front axle, but everything else blends in well

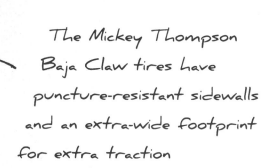

1. **LED spotlight**
2. **Front nudge bar**
3. **Skid plate**
4. **Hood air duct**
5. **Headlight protector**
6. **Cooling duct**
7. **Rear spoiler**
8. **Roll bar**
9. **Rear fender extension**
10. **Front fender extension**
11. **Twin-damper front suspension**
12. **Off-road tyre**

The Mickey Thompson Baja Claw tires have puncture-resistant sidewalls and an extra-wide footprint for extra traction

MODIFIED REBEL

'THE REBEL LOOKED SCARIER THAN THE CREATURES
BY THE TIME WE'D FINISHED THE MODS'

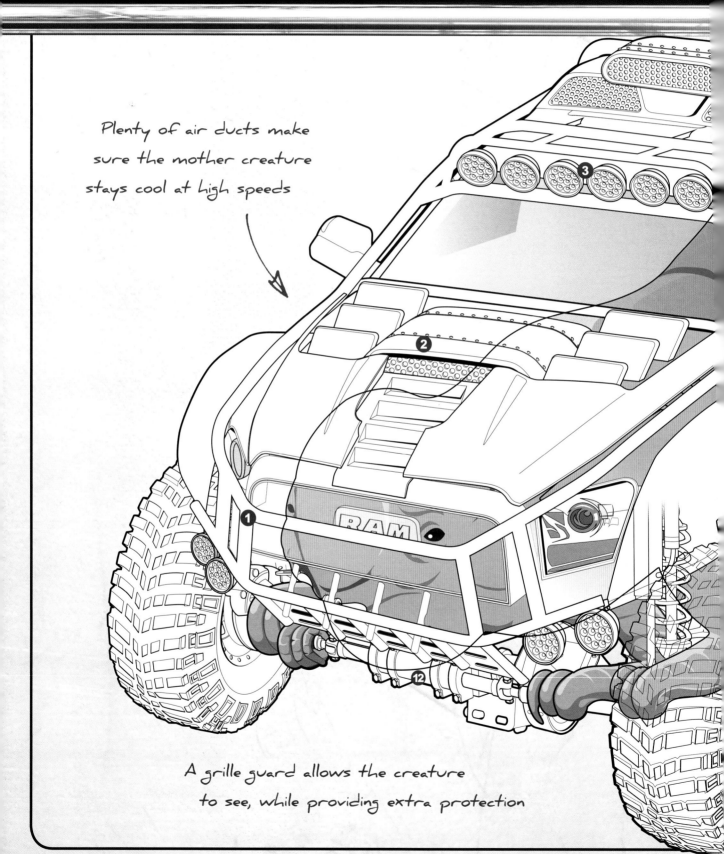

Plenty of air ducts make
sure the mother creature
stays cool at high speeds

RAM

A grille guard allows the creature
to see, while providing extra protection

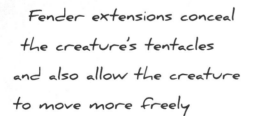

1. Front nudge bar
2. Hood cooling duct
3. LED spotlights
4. Cabin air ducts
5. Rear spoiler
6. Spare wheel
7. Roll cage
8. Rear fender extension
9. Air duct
10. Rock slider rail/step
11. Front fender extension
12. Steering rack

Fender extensions conceal the creature's tentacles and also allow the creature to move more freely

Transcript from Central Dispatch, Sentinel County Sheriff's Department

Dispatcher: Sheriff's department, how can I help you?

Ken Calloway: Hey, it's Ken Calloway here, on Old Cutler Road.

Dispatcher: Hey, Ken. Mike Martinous here.

Ken Calloway: Hey, Mike. Listen, a bunch of trucks just raced over my land, right into the wheat fields.

Dispatcher: You're in the fields now?

Ken Calloway: No, in my house, saw them through the window.

Dispatcher: They were racing? Can you still see them?

Ken Calloway: No, they're gone now.

Dispatcher: What kind of trucks were they?

Ken Calloway: Well, they looked like monster trucks.

Dispatcher: Monster trucks?

Ken Calloway: Yeah, I know that probably sounds odd, but I...

Dispatcher: No, Ken, listen, we're actually on the lookout for a large truck that...

Ken Calloway: You mean the one in yesterday's paper, causing accidents in town?

Dispatcher: Yeah, that's right. But you said you saw a bunch of trucks? How many?

Ken Calloway: Well first three went by, and then a bunch of black ones followed them, heading for the woods.

Dispatcher: All of them were monster trucks?

Ken Calloway: Well, the first three sure looked like it. I'm not so sure about the black trucks. But they looked big too.

Dispatcher: Okay, Ken, I'm sending a deputy over to your place now, and I'll also call Sheriff Lovick, let him know which way the trucks are headed. You stay put, don't go outside, just wait for the deputy.

Ken Calloway: Okay, Mike. Thanks and good luck to you.

CANYON SHOWDOWN

Bill had learned that the creatures had a "hive intelligence," which meant that Creatch's knowledge about how to power a truck was immediately passed on to his parents. Creatch and I drove the Old Mutt, while Meredith and the mother creature drove the Rebel, and Bill and the father creature drove the Power Wagon.

Too bad that Burke and his team were experienced trackers. We were still making a run for the area where Bill said the creatures could return to their underground home when Burke's crew caught up with us. We had to climb an incredibly steep grade to try to get away from them, but even then, they kept on coming.

What happened next? Plenty. A lot of rough stuff went down in a canyon, but I'm not about to spill the beans on everything for one big reason, which is this: I want to protect my friends, my human friends as well as the creatures.

But I'll say this much. Without Mr. Weathers, Bill Dowd, Meredith, Sam Geldon, and also an assist from a certain law-enforcement officer, our little adventure might have had a very different ending.

TRIPP COLEY

I've known Tripp Coley for a while, and I have to say that before this whole situation with the oil-eating creatures, and these so-called "monster trucks," I didn't think Tripp cared about anything except maybe getting a set of wheels that would take him out of Sentinel County. I never got the impression he was even too thoughtful about what that set of wheels looked like, just so long as they got him as far away as possible. I don't mean to sound like a judgmental old fogey, just telling it like I saw it.

But something happened to Tripp, something that changed him, and for the better. It wasn't just one thing that affected him, more like a bunch of things that happened within a short time. One day, Tripp seemed happiest when he was crushing cars at my garage. Next thing I know, he actually cares about the lives of others!

I'm hardly perfect. I've made plenty of mistakes. Haven't we all? The thing to keep in mind is that we all have opportunities in our lives to do the right thing, to help others instead of doing something selfish. We all should try hard to do the right things more often.

What's the future hold for Tripp and his friends? Will he and Creatch ever take the Old Mutt for another spin? I have no idea. But I'm glad Tripp and Creatch found each other when they did, and not just because they made life more interesting.

They made things better.

WEATHERS

This book ROCKS!
I'm definitely sending it to
the editors at Haynes Manuals!

Sam

Writer & Artist Credits:

Ryder Windham is the author of over 70 books, including Haynes *Star Wars Millennium Falcon Owner's Workshop Manual* and *Star Wars Imperial Death Star Owner's Workshop Manual*. He resides in Providence, Rhode Island, which is routinely listed on various insurance companies' top ten lists for worst drivers in America. He often wishes he owned a monster truck.

Ian Moores is an award-winning artist with over 30 years of experience in illustration, design and information graphics. His work has appeared in numerous books, magazines and newspapers, including the *Sunday Times*, and graces the covers and pages of a diverse range of Haynes Manuals, from the *Apollo 13 Owner's Workshop Manual* to the *Zombie Survival Manual*!

Image Credits: